Skoob Books Publishing Ltd., **London** presents a new imprint:

Skoob *PACIFICA* is contributing to World Literatures in English, disseminating regional literatures of the Pacific Rim and promoting understanding between continents.

At the turn of the last century, Europe developed a penchant for novels set in lands afar which had a tendency to look **at** the colonies whereas the Postcolonials view from within themselves, experimenting with the deviation from tradition and affirming the aesthetic of the sublime as against an aesthetic of the beautiful.

As the *fin-de-millenium* approaches, the colonies have a voice of their own, a new *genre* has developed. Ironically, this diachrony is written in the language of the Imperialist. Behind the facade of tropical, sandy beaches and factories of video games lies the cross-cultural and interliterary tradition of two continents.

Skoob *PACIFICA: THE EMPIRE WRITES BACK !*

D1546345

SKOOB *Pacifica*

Joint Series Editors: C.Y. Loh & I.K. Ong

SKOOB *Pacifica*

No. 2015

MONSOON HISTORY

Selected Poems from:
Modern Secrets
and
No Man's Grove
with the complete
Crossing The Peninsula
winner of the Commonwealth Poetry Prize
1980

Shirley Geok-lin Lim

MONSOON HISTORY
Selected Poems

Introduction
by
Professor Laurel Means
McMaster University

SKOOB BOOKS PUBLISHING
LONDON

Introduction   © Laurel Means
Cover Design   © I.K.Ong
Published in 1994 by
SKOOB BOOKS PUBLISHING LTD
Skoob PACIFICA Series
11a-17 Sicilian Avenue
off Southampton Row and
Bloomsbury Square
London WC1A 2QH
Fax: 71- 404 4398

ISBN 1 871438 44 6

Agents:
Skoob Books (Malaysia) Sdn Bhd
11 Jalan Telawi Tiga, Bangsar Baru
59100 Kuala Lumpur
Tel/Fax: 603-255 2686

Atrium Publishing Group
11270 Clayton Creek Road
Lower Lake
CA. 95457
Tel: 1-707-995 3906
Fax: 1-707-995 1814

Graham Brash (Pte) Ltd
32 Gul Drive
Singapore 2262
Tel: 65-861 1335, 65-862 0437 Fax: 65-861 4815

Typeset by Pearly Kok. Tel/Fax: 603-255 2686
Printed in Malaysia by POLYGRAPHIC. Fax: 603-905 1553
Colour Separation by Universal Litho Fax: 603-717 7527

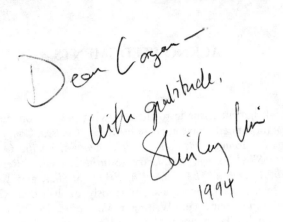

Dear Logan —
with gratitude,
Stanley Liu
1994

To *those* at home and abroad

ACKNOWLEDGMENTS

Acknowledgment is made to the following publications in which some of these poems have appeared: *ARIEL, Chelsea, Commentary, Contact/II, Homegrown II, Kunapipi, Meanjin, Pacific Quarterly Moana, Sibyl, Singa, Solidarity, Southeast Asian Review of English, Tenggara, The Journal of Ethnic Studies,* and *Westerly.* The selected poems were also previously published in *Crossing the Peninsula* (Heinemann Writing in Asia Series, 1980), *No Man's Grove* (English Department National University of Singapore Shell Series, 1985, and *Modern Secrets* (Dangaroo Press, 1989).

The author thanks Laurel Braswell-Means, Anna Rutherford and Ike Ong for their encouragement.

CONTENTS

INTRODUCTION

Shirley Geok-lin Lim brings a uniqueness to her poetry which neither past nor contemporary, Asian nor Western, American nor Asian American writers can claim. Lim's writing emphatically reflects the complex mosaic of her world: one originating in the rich context of Peranaken Malaysia — that combination of Malay and Chinese tradition associated with Malacca on the southwest coast of Malaysia. Her world moreover confronts the apparent incongruities of Western colonial education and its transition to the harsh perplexities of North American life. Born in Malacca before Malaysian independence in 1957, educated first in a Roman Catholic convent school, then receiving a B.A. (first class Honours English) from the University of Malaya in Kuala Lumpur, she came to the United States for a M.A. and Ph.D. from Brandeis University, and stayed, first to teach at Westchester College, New York, eventually to become Professor of English and Women's Studies at the University of California in Santa Barbara, her current position.

The present structure of this new edition of Shirley Geok-lin Lim's selected poems, including all the poems in her Commonwealth Poetry Prize award collection *Crossing the Peninsula and Other Poems* (1980), her second collection *No Man's Grove* (1985), and third book, *Modern Secrets* (1989), is intended to reflect such biographical circumstances, to convey thematically the unique phenomena which lie behind her poetic vision. At the same time, these poems serve as witness to a highly individual response to that vision, one couched in a skilful artistry which often masks profound insights and biting satire in a language at once lucid and succinct. Most importantly, the poems illustrate that the universal qualities of Lim's vision do not limit her to the Peranaken or the Chinese American or the American cultural contexts. Rather, they clearly signify the voice of a poet speaking out in society, articulating the wonders of nature, the mysteries of creativity, the mutability of time, the emotions of love and hate, the pangs of memory, the survival of will, the survival of women. The poems of this edition are arranged in six sections more or less chronologically aligned with Lim's personal history, although not, of course, in the order in which they were written. Their selection is intended to be only representative of the complex subject matter and craftsmanship of Lim's poetry. For readers familiar with Lim's work, they will facilitate re-reading, an act rendered difficult because of the paucity if not unavailability of the earlier collections. For readers unfamiliar, they are intended to introduce Lim's outstanding poetic achievement.

The first section, *Bukit China* (Malay 'China Hill,' a place-name in Malacca), introduces in its title poem the theme of return to the land of origin and especially to its associations with a still more distant ancestry — the 'view' from this 'hill' looks toward China:

> Bless me, spirits, I am returning.
> Stone marking my father's bones,
> I light the joss. A dead land."

The loss is not only father/Malaysia, not only the Chinese traditions of a Peranaken society; rather the poem describes lost roots symbolized by the father, roots now severed by guilt imposed by time and diaspora. Other poems in this section present those memories in different guises. The rich exotic images of the "Lotus" grow pale in a memory circumscribed by "Atlantic mist;" a contrast is made between the "Mother" in "her grandfather's garden," lush in "red-blossomed banana, yellow / Chempedak," and the present barrenness of a foreign modernity. Yet the harshness of women's life in that traditional Chinese world of patriarchal hegemony is poignantly described in the poem "Pantoun for Chinese Women," when the mother, in giving birth to a female child, "cannot bear the waste" of infanticide.

In the second section, *Monsoon History,* Lim sites her memories more specifically in Malacca, "Malay-ness," and childhood. This is nowhere so well evoked as in the title poem. Here images of a tropical monsoon envelope in its "down-pour/ing rain" and pervasive wetness a household filled with mother and father, with security, with history and cultural layers:

> Nonya and baba sit at home.
> This was forty years ago.

> Sarong-wrapped they counted
> Silver paper for the dead.
> Portraits of grandfathers
> Hung always in the parlour.

The images of this scene hang suspended, silent, "Like sleepers rocked in the pantun, / Sheltered by Malacca."

Taking up similar monsoon images in "Crossing the Peninsula," the poet reminiscences a childhood on the shore, "where we went footed as crabs," a the season when "boats come home to shelter" (a similar thought in "Monsoon History") and

> We dream like grey gulls blown inland,
> Or as one-eyed ships, blown, espying
> The bright-shelled peninsula.

The 'peninsula' thus becomes a trope of identity with a Malaysian past, 'crossing' it symbolizes its loss and the necessity for "espying" it only through memory, as if in a dream. "We cannot enter their dream" is the opening thought of "No Man's Grove,' which describes the mergence of sea and jungle, "sailors, knee-deep in padi," that ambivalent land/seascape creating an ambivalent identity and forcing the poet to "walk between water and land."

Imagining a physical return from beyond that peninsula to contemplate a Malaccan childhood is the theme of several other poems in this section. "Reminder to the Young" cautions "Don't overlook the old gods" in evaluating their role in a society which believed in them. Their Taoist rituals are remembered in "my mother's house," where belief always must give way to reason. Religious belief provides the theme of two other returns in "Christmas in Exile" and "Returning to the Missionary School." In the former, the poet remembers "A colonial Christmas and second-hand nostalgia." The contrast between this seasonal association and the fact that the Christ must now be "born in odd conditions," where "O silent, holy night" is sung "beneath / The clear hot equatorial sky," brings with it not so much a contrast as a sinister parallel with contemporary politics (a veiled allusion, as well, to contemporary Malaysian ethnic policies) and the nature of life itself: here,

> . . . as everywhere, even to the hour of birth,
> Soldiers keep watch. Frivolity
> Is circumscribed by birth, by death.

"Returning to the Missionary School" establishes its central paradigm around another irony of the Asian/Western religious dichotomy. The town's daughters in damp pinafores contrast with the "red-lipped hibiscus [that] stick / Thick pistils in the watery air"; the nuns, "Breastless women stuffed with God," attempt tuneless to teach music to "so many singing children." Finally, the old family house in "Visiting Malacca" is explored and found to be as the poet remembered, "But not itself, not empty, clean." Gone are the presences of a house "dark with opium," with "children running crowded / Through passageways." Yet still, "something of China remains," and we are brought back to thoughts of earlier poems like "Bukit China" with images of "Gold-leaf carving" or the "Cracked flowered tiles grandfather / Brought shining in crates from China." Images of Malacca serve only to awaken the poet to a reality in which identity assumes an indeterminant state. The peninsula has been crossed — but where is the point of reference now?

A point of reference comes in the third section, *Dedicated to Confucius Plaza*. With a play in the title poem upon the 'confusion' of 'Confucius' values, the poet attempts to evaluate her 'crossing over' into a North American context. Once again implying the view from "Bukit China," she looks out upon

> . . . the East River
> Where the air is cold as
> On Tung Shen Mountains.

The city of New York, too, is a mountain, "made of Asia, / Europe and Africa." Almost as an automaton, she practices *li*, eats "pop, crackle, snap," and thus finds it not "hard to be / An Asian-American Chinee." In "To Li Po," Lim contrasts the vision of a kindred poet whose Classical Chinese vision was never obscured by having "to live among / Foreign devils," whose vision remained integral to the world around him. His stories only serve to "Stir griefs of dispersion," to remind her that she can no longer speak his tongue with ease nor envision his ricefields. Yet the poet dreams in Chinese in "Modern Secrets," a dream of a "sallow child" eating "rice from its ricebowl," and identity is further confused in "Identity no Longer," in which the notion of "Citizenness of the world" becomes a hollow mockery in being imposed largely through the promises of a Western education: "gruesome Eliot," "ponderous Pound," "Willy whisking his Irish horn-pipe," and "stern J.V. [Cunningham]" catch her short, waving "only her papers."

American identity is contemplated in its larger sense in several poems of this section. There is a universal aspect to it expressed, for example, in "Translation from Other Languages." Yet in "The Mind of the Beholder," the autumn landscape of maples, "white towns and houses / Shingled with golden leaves," serves only as a bitter emblem of the "American dream," smoke as the "bitter scent of country / Reminding of lavender, herbs, elm-tree."

"The Windscreen's Speckled View" and "American Driving" pointedly summarize essential conflicts between Asian and American identities through identity with the mother, who represents that genetic and gender link with place and tradition — the "woman there and this woman here," as Lim describes it in "The Windscreen's Speckled View." This is a five-part poem (one of Lim's longest) describing a daughter's return to a dying mother after a fifteen years' absence, throughout her journey laden with feelings of guilt, the inability to grieve, yet eventually "amazed by tears" at the mother's failures and the daughter's rejection of her. The lines "Drawing nearer to you, rounding / the figure, yet I am losing the race" play upon "race" in the sense of time and ancestry, while the final line, "These asiatic reveries disturb some wavering sense," summarizes return of the poet's mind to that paradigmatic site of Malaysian identity. The mother also draws the daughter back in mid-journey in "American Driving." Driving through the "caucasian countryside," wanting "to stop / And look at life," she cannot do so, even when

> . . . My mother's hand is reaching
> From fat autumn clouds. 'Where
> Are you going? Who are you?'

The poet's dilemma is clearly that such enigmas are no longer solvable.

Section IV, *A Life of Imagination,* summarizes Lim's responses to mainly Western culture. Its relevance already challenged in such poems as "Returning to the Missionary School," these poems consider such poets as Marianne Moore and Whitman, such painters as Cezanne and Munch within the more significant context of the nature of creativity itself. Such a context offers an important *credo* for Lim's own view of her art. Lines from the title poem, "A Life of Imagination," could, in fact, describe her own work: possessing images "in vision," the poet calls them forth,

> . . . So dreading
> In mind, his poetry grew
> Whole, packed,

or in the poem "In Praise of a Master," the maker is

> Master in his craft, he'd come
> To finished form, perceived
> What words may give.

"On Hearing a Woman Poet Read" offers further insights into *poeisis;* the poet asks,

> . . . Are you our sister whose words
> Awaken in rooms of strangers to know
> Yourself?

She considers the medium of art to probe the hidden recesses of the unconscious ("Science Fiction" and "To Marianne Moore") and the ability of the painter to perceive and capture in time the hidden essences of life ("The Painter, Munch" and "Thoughts on a Cezanne Still-Life"). In "An Immigrant Looks at Whitman," Lim, through the created natural images of poetry, makes a rare attempt to bring her Asian and American worlds into harmony with one another:

> But, for you, bring golden pheasant,
> Goldenrod, my Asia, my America.
> I fish in the Great Lakes inwards,
> Forsaking gods for leeches and wild pansy.

Section V, *The Elements,* indeed re-creates many aspects of the natural world, of life and the absence of life. Summarized in the title poem, the poet compares her total sublimation of self by another to the sleep of winter, "when life goes under / Radically," embracing darkness, when the very silence allows one to hear

> Order in the times, forfeiting
> Leaf stir and wood shadows
> To find again stone scraping against root
> And earth, water, air.

The wonders of nature are seen in its creations, whether animal — "Land-Turtle," "Crocodile," "Panther," or vegetable: "Brinjal" (eggplant), "Cactus." Yet there are deeper significations, often suggestive of Blake. Animals may be seen as threatening, with humankind unable to understand or control the primitive forces motivating them. There is a sinister aspect to the "contempt" in the land-turtle's "button eyes;" to the fate that coincides the crocodile's hunger, "its passion," with the presence of "the warm body of a bather;" to the "wired force" in the panther's head, a "bowl in which passions hiss / like acids and sulphurs." The panther is female, in her enforced sullenness and immobility a metaphor for female-kind.

Nature exerts a wondrous beauty and force in "Cactus" and "Shells." "Shells" remind us once again of the Malaysian coast, their beauty "lovely, fished from Sabah sea. / Jewels of water." But their tragedy is to become souvenirs for sale, objects for maids to dust, collectors' items. Snatched from their natural setting, "Trawled by strings / Of human-kind," they have become merely "dead trappings / Of beauty . . . Abandoned to light and placeless; bereft." Again, it is Lim's sense of order, of belonging, of "place" that thematically shapes these poems.

The final and longest section of this collection, *Women's Dreams,* represents one of Shirley Geok-lin Lim's major concerns:

gender. The theme has already been demonstrated in earlier poems like "Bukit China," "Dedicated to Confucius Plaza," "The Windscreen's Speckled View," "The Elements," "Panther," and many others (and generally shapes her short stories). The poems of this section speak further of women in their many roles, for example, as mother, daughter, wife, prostitute, and of their relationships, both negative and positive, to men. The over-all tone is one of longing and cynicism: longing for greater freedom from the traditions of patriarchal hegemony and social constraint (both Asian and American), cynicism concerning the likelihood of change and uncompromised happiness. Several poems describe how these factors shape the roles women must play. The title poem, "Women's Dreams," describes women's delight "in the effort to fit / Being Mother Nature and our own creation," and humorously outlines the strategies to "match wits / Because we have not known dominion." "Queens" also describes the "magic" women must weave, through "witchweaver(s)" Scheherazade and Penelope coalesced into prostitute and stripteaser, "A net of stories to catch a king." "Mannequins" presents women as "images of surface . . . not filled / by others," whose "perfect circuity" is only an illusion, "Reflection / Of Narcissus clothed in perfection," and loved only by women through adoption of an image imposed upon them by men.

"I Look for Women" sets the theme for a number of poems in this section which examine not so much the roles created for women but those which women either patently reject or seek to change. "Where are they" the poet here asks, those who can fulfil such challenges and bring meaning to their lives? "Birth, Sex, Death" and "Inventing Mothers" summarize the potential emptiness of women's lives (there where sex is sold, where mothers are made), "In Cities Some Old Women" describes the loneliness that comes with denial of identity. "Danny Boy" attempts to resist women's feelings of fear and helplessness against macho-male threat.

Women's feelings in these poems are generated by a number of concerns. Lim expresses them through different techniques, whether through the precise scene-setting of "Danny Boy" or the metaphor of "The Tent." Often such feelings use the symbolic language of dreams, as in "Modern Secrets," or speak through enforced female silence, as in "Panther." In most, ironic humour points the meaning.

Technically, Lim's poems reflect their extensive thematic variety. Mainly written in free verse, their stanzaic variations nevertheless are carefully crafted to reinforce subject and effect, often to suggest or even parody more traditional Western forms, for example the sonnet in "Danny Boy" and "Translation from Other Languages," or the four-line English ballad stanza in "American Driving." The latter poem also demonstrates how Lim often uses assonance, the last stanza especially effective in its "error / narrow / forever / tomorrow" to remind us that the word "yesterday" introduces the poem, and to summarize the theme of conflict between past, present, and future desire. Imbedded rhyming couplets may serve to arrest diegesis, as in "To Li Po." The repetition of triplet rhymes (aba) in "Family Album" reinforces the poem's paradigm of repeated male hegemony.

Certainly unique in Lim's prosody is her use of the *pantoun,* a traditional Malay verse form. "Pantoun for Chinese Women" follows the requirements precisely. There, eight stanzas of four-lines each interlock rhyme schemes by repeating the last rhyme of each stanza in reverse order: abab / baba / acac / cdcd / dcdc / cdcd / dede / eded. The form seems highly appropriate for the poem's theme of binding, stifling, repetitious tradition.

Within her imagery, Lim demonstrates a number of striking features. An acute, sensitive observation of nature is everywhere evident, whether in describing "sky / With swift light changing to rain" in "Crossing the Peninsula," or the details of "Shells" —

> . . . smooth
> And rosy conch designed in stipples,
> Pearly bands not pink nor any color
> Mixed by mind.

At the same time, images reflecting nature's beauty may generate similes creating unexpected conceits, as in "Brinjal":

> . . . impenetrable
> skin like first sex; shiny as spit,
> as slippery,

or the shocking nightmarish horror of "A giant thing, half-bird, half-octopus, / With beak to tear and flapping wings" ("Science Fiction").

Where, then, is Shirley Geok-lin Lim's poetry to be placed in the English literary canon? It could claim a rightful place in post-colonial Malaysian writing in English. Nevertheless, two obvious comparisons present central differences. Unlike Mohammed Haji Salleh, whose largest corpus of English poetry was written from the 1960s to the 1980s, she does not share his special Malay vision of the natural world, the *kampong* ('village'), one which also finds expression in its language: one has only to compare Salleh's poem "tropics," for example, to understand how similar Malaysian shoreline images can inspire very different responses. Ee Tiang Hong, like Lim from the Peranakan background which produced such nostalgic "return" poems as "Herren Street, Malacca," after higher education in England, the United States, and Australia also emigrated. From 1976 until his death in 1990, he produced poems which might be considered part of the Australian post-colonial canon. Ee Tiang Hong's Australian life, however, never had the profound impact upon his work as Lim's American experiences have had upon hers.

For this reason, Shirley Geok-lin Lim has also a legitimate claim within the Chinese American canon. Like Maxine Hong Kingston and Amy Tan, she represents an important voice in breaking the long silence of an ethnic group, in articulating concerns of "place" and "gender." But certainly, too, Lim's work over the past decade unquestionably attests to her importance as both critic and writer within the larger canon of contemporary English literature, whether criticism, fiction, or poetry.

Laurel Means
McMaster University
Hamilton, Canada

FOREWORD

Learning English

A change of heart.
An English phrase, a Western idea.
I couldn't understand
its meaning. A child,
I knew hearts did not change —
grew older unfaithful
forgetful, but were the same
father, mother.
Unfaithful
forgetful, but still father mother.

It wasn't like changing
shoes, one pair of shoes
for leather heels
tap-dancing semaphores
of excessive meaning.
Or like simple translation:
ditditdit dahdahdah ditditdit.
It was like learning
to let go and to hold on:
a slow braking, shifting
gears, an engine
of desire on a downhill
slope, momentum of vocabularies
carrying the child
to foreign countries,
to families of strangers,
an orphanage of mind,
and technologies of empire.

It was more like cry,
a beloved country, and
see, traveler, on a hill,
by the wall, exchanging
what must be changed
forever, good-bye, farewell,
the different words working,
to say what is
unchangeable. Say, father mother.

Shirley Geok-lin Lim

BUKIT CHINA

Bukit China

Bless me, spirits, I am returning.
Stone marking my father's bones,
I light the joss. A dead land.
On noon steepness smoke ascends
Briefly. Country is important,
Is important. This knowledge I know
If it will rise with smoke, with the dead.

He did not live for my returning.
News came after burial.
I did not put on straw, black,
Gunny-sack, have not fastened
Grief on shoulder, walked mourning
Behind, pouring grief before him,
Not submitted to his heart.

This then must be enough, salt light
For nights, remembering bamboo
And bats cleared in his laughter.
My father's daughter, I pour
No brandy before memory.
But labour, constantly labour,
Bearing sunwards grave bitter smoke.

Lotus

It waits to be discovered:
Purity drifting on morning water.
Selangor ditch or Atlantic mist,
The pressure of waking is
The same. Bird whistle, cry,
The same disenchantment, only
Colder, grey in sky water.

Not weedy float of flower,
Etch of purple, pink or yellow
Overtaken by noon — the blister
Of lotus in klongs. Defer
The exotic; these tropic decorations
Pale as do winter description.
Only what is is the flower.

Mother

Mother is toothless, sag-skinned,
Coconut round and brown with scar.
She knew pantuns, on Mandi Safar,
Sarong knotted modestly,
Fell into the sea, milk-fleshed young.
Ungainly now, unstrung,
She cannot stand heat, lies snoring
Under circling breezes.

In her grandfather's garden
Extraordinary fruit yearned:
Red-blossomed banana, yellow
Chempedak. She washed carefully
Eggshells to cap the spiky pandan.
Leached landscape bruised by sun,
He made it magical
With edible bushes.

Sand clean from his garden rubbed
Into soles, penetrated blood
Like gold-yellow seeds. They cling
To our feet. She sits on the floor
By Scandinavian sofa
Blond as her gold-washed ring; rising
She shuffles to the refrigerator
In search of Malacca sweets.

Pantoun for Chinese Women

"At present, the phenomena of butchering, drowning
and leaving to die female infants have been very serious."
(**The People's Daily**, Peking, March 3rd, 1983)

They say a child with two mouths is no good.
In the slippery wet, a hollow space,
Smooth, gumming, echoing wide for food.
No wonder my man is not here at his place.

In the slippery wet, a hollow space,
A slit narrowly sheathed within its hood.
No wonder my man is not here at his place:
He is digging for the dragon jar of soot.

That slit narrowly sheathed within its hood!
His mother, squatting, coughs by the fire's blaze
While he digs for the dragon jar of soot.
We had saved ashes for a hundred days.

His mother, squatting, coughs by the fire's blaze.
The child kicks against me mewing like a flute.
We had saved ashes for a hundred days.
Knowing, if the time came, that we would.

The child kicks against me crying like a flute
Through its two weak mouths. His mother prays
Knowing when the time comes that we would,
For broken clay is never set in glaze.

Through her two weak mouths his mother prays.
She will not pluck the rooster nor serve its blood,
For broken clay is never set in glaze:
Women are made of river sand and wood.

She will not pluck the rooster nor serve its blood.
My husband frowns, pretending in his haste
Women are made of river sand and wood.
Milk soaks the bedding. I cannot bear the waste.

My husband frowns, pretending in his haste.
Oh clean the girl, dress her in ashy soot!
Milk soaks our bedding, I cannot bear the waste.
They say a child with two mouth is no good.

The Debt

All night the cocks crow in my head.
I am tired. My eyes will not close,
Counting the dollars I owe,
Children in the broken house,
And promises never made
Which bind tighter than sleep.

I count the children, squeezed bony
Faces, all sisters and brothers,
My burden, stretching pastwards to dead
Rotting fathers and mothers.
Pinched, careless as poverty,
They lie on thin cots, to whom each night's
An end, each morning for nothing.

The stink of suffering,
Love without rescue, grinds salt,
Grinds my heart. Awake in bed,
Under my heavy feather
Coverlet, fixed on darkness,
I count myself, all that is owed.

Dulang-Washer

The dulang-washer, squinting like a witch,
Squats with rag-wrapped head and begging-bowl.
The sun mocks her with false gold.
Still she bows her head acquiescently.

How will she die? In memory of movement,
The monotonous rhythm of search
And discarding. Changeless streams and gravel
Will dim her sight, exchanging gold-dust
For rocks in the head. No glamour of departure
Enshrines her travel, the shift
From landscape to landscape a meagre drift.

Arak

A name of wine, to make
virtuous women drunk:
you perch on long legs, one
staunch as a soldier tapping
in *romvong* rhythm, the other
your tender child, clubbed
and forbidden. How tall
you stood leaning on the lame foot.
What gawky Northern warrior
walked down Chao Prathaya
centuries ago to glow
in your pure eyes? Drunk
on cheap Balinese beer
and Siamese love-songs,
yet you are chained to your
clubbed pride, your Thai soul.

Opium

To invite,
to open the door,
to lift the latch, saying,
Come in.
Little stirs,
flourishes of dust,
quick bright flare
of dry bark
gone almost without
warmth.
This fire is not good
for anything.

First and third uncles lit
burnished pipes.
Hummingbirds of paradise
honed in their ears
dripping with honey.
Smoke dragons drew in
rainbow tails and shed
scales of money.
Their chests closed in,
the smooth, hairless, yellow
skins of Chinese babies
without a mark.

The Chinese Painter

Of a backward ancient country
I dream. Where wind sits in stale eddies,
Standing water, ripe as
Urinals, pools under moon,
White-faced, a distant lady.
Long limp marsh grass
Floats like drowning hair.

Rising, I paint the scene
Swirling palely; leave
Transparent paper showing in
White reflection of my eyes:
That is, spontaneous sight!
Such chill sorrowing ghosts
Move among us in the night.

Sugar-Cane

Once, we are told, the massacres came:
Women, children, seized by hair, slaughtered,
Running everywhere into blood and death, the same
Dark men with metal arms killing, killing, the dead
Like rags too beggared for burying. And the men,
Those who had not run into blood and death, hid
In fields under roots of padi, the muddy water
Of life shaking, shaking, to be rooted out then
By the same dark men shearing alike the plant
And flesh. Oh to be like air and light,
So easily swallowed, like tender grain in slant
Of steel! Only in hills where canes grew thick,
Crouched in gold and yellow shadows, where sight
Of darkness is thrown for a moment, the sick
And timorous escaped that day.
                                        Still here today,
We have not forgotten these casual stalks, slender
Saviours on which we have fattened. And the dark men
In their bloody work, who will come yet if we stay,
Or if we run and are running everywhere.

Epitaph

I

Begotten with a brood of brothers, led
A noisy early life, she later fed
A solitary, solipsistic head,
And never knew its cause till she was dead.

II

She could have married and never did.
Of the men and women with whom she hid,
Some live on in respected past.
She has herself, and she has dust.

III

Here lies a woman who chose to leave
Home, husband, children, and the weave
Of poverty. She lived alone. The grief
We record upon her death is brief.

MONSOON HISTORY

Monsoon History

The air is wet, soaks
Into mattresses, and curls
In apparitions of smoke.
Like fat white slugs furled
Among the timber,
Or silver fish tunnelling
The damp linen covers
Of schoolbooks, or walking
Quietly like centipedes,
The air walking everywhere
On its hundred feet
Is filled with the glare
Of tropical water.

Again we are taken over
By clouds and rolling darkness.
Small snails appear
Clashing their timid horns
Among the morning glory
Vines.
      Drinking milo,
Nonya and baba sit at home.
This was forty years ago.
Sarong-wrapped they counted
Silver paper for the dead.
Portraits of grandfathers
Hung always in the parlour.

Reading Tennyson, at six
p.m. in pajamas,

Listening to down-pour-
ing rain: the air ticks
With gnats, black spiders fly,
Moths sweep out of our rooms
Where termites built
Their hills of eggs and queens zoom
In heat. We wash our feet
For bed, watch mother uncoil
Her snake hair, unbuckle
The silver mesh around her waist,
Waiting for father pacing
The sand as fishers pull
From the Straits after monsoon.

The air is still, silent
Like sleepers rocked in the pantun,
Sheltered by Malacca.
This was forty years ago,
When nyonya married baba.

When

When I was a child, I would watch the spray
Break phosphorescence at my feet then run away.
There was so much sea, always rhythmically
And gently pulling to the horizon.
There was the enormous starry clarity
Of sky and, sharply, carried upon
The breeze, the smells of pines and salty sea.
It was a child's preoccupation
To stare at the yellow coin of moon,
To crumble pine needles between thumb and finger,
Not thinking anything particular, to linger,
Watching the trees bend in the wind, sea dance,
Till you knew it was time to be home soon,
And straightaway left with no backward glance.

Crossing the Peninsula

First, the sea, blue heart pulsing,
Spilling stars, nuts, and sand
On Tanjong Bunga. Rocks, their sides ringed
By wave, where we went footed as crabs,
Toes like white fish washed under,
Hunting shorewards for sweet oysters
And mother-of-pearl. Then sky
With swift light changing to rain.
The humming breakers push by,
Recede, run in again
Through days, through years. It is monsoon
Climate, the migrating season
When nets and boats come home to shelter.
And all night the water beats heavily.
Salt falls from our hair and traps
In a dream the sailors motionlessly
Rocking in the eye of the moon.
We dream like grey gulls blown inland,
Or as one-eyed ships, blown, espying
The bright-shelled peninsula.

Tropical Colours

Peet! goes the bird.
The branch isn't silver.
It is black, grey, blue, green,
all colours of trees
in nature.

The colours of nature
remembered are grey
The mind is cold silver,
pewter dull. What an effort
to polish it.

Remembered pieces shine
like silver paper
glinting cigarette paper
from childhood.
I always believed
there was silver in them.
I knew I wasn't supposed to:
only paper after all,
smelling horribly
of tobacco.
It crumpled easily.

I found it
in coffee-shops
with spittoons
under every table.
Marble tops cold
in tropical afternoons,

stained yellow.
I thought they were
pieces of floor.

And father, always
in a good mood
except when he was mad.
He had nine children
and wanted us all.
I wonder, did I
pay him back?
Where did he go?
The warm air circulates
with ceiling fans above
the clerical child
still clutching
silver pieces
among Dutch-red offices.

My Father

My father said, "Please finish your studies.
This is what I want you to do." Nervous,
I remember, as though he's raised his fist,
And I'm cowed again with misery.

And I will, father, to make your heart swell,
Learn dead languages, music, numbers.
You'll have a daughter to show the neighbours,
To wink at; to keep your years well.

When younger, my father had wanted
Everything, if he could afford it,
To make me happy. I am sorry
Then I had not learned enough to lie.

My Father's Sadness

My father's sadness appears in my dreams.
His young body is dying of responsibility.
So many men and women march out of his mouth
each time he opens his heart for fullness,
he is shot down; so many men and women
like dragons' teeth rising in the instance
of his lifetime. He is an oriental. He claims
paternity. But in his dreams he is a young body
with only his life before him.

My father's sadness masks my face. It is hard
to see through his tears, his desires drum in my chest.
I tense like a young man with a full moon
and no woman in sight. My father broke
with each child, finer and finer, the clay
of his body crumbling to a drizzle of silicone
in the hour-glass. How hard it is
to be a father, a bull under the axle,
the mangrove netted by lianas, the host
perishing of its lavishness.

Potions

Bitter tea,
hot or cold,
equally good
for chest pains,
loose bowels,
chills, fevers,
sore throats,
coughs in the night,
and other body ailments.
He drank thermos-flasks
but did not recover.

Ginger-root
awakens hunger,
overcomes langour,
combats age,
heats the blood
and revitalizes
its motions.
He ate ginger
but lost weight;
haloed with pain,
grew light like a child.

Morphine pills,
take one a day.
Take one when needed
or every so often.
Like yellow wax
dissolving,

he sheds hope
for his life.
His children meet
to bless his bones.

Christmas in Exile

Christmas is coming and I think of home:
A colonial Christmas and second-hand nostalgia
As simple as home-made cottonwool snow,
Paste holly and a cheap plastic conifer.
Where Christ is born in odd conditions,
To customary churches and celebration.
O silent, holy night, we sing, beneath
The clear hot equatorial sky.
Where, as everywhere, even to the hour of birth,
Soldiers keep watch. Frivolity
Is circumscribed by birth, by death.

Fear

I am afraid to study
Any more the past,
Breathing slowly along
The nervous edge of crying.
All things bring me back
To this small place
Of pity and terror
Which so circles me
I cannot run. Seeing
There is no place,
It is best perhaps,
Entirely, to disappear.

Reminder to the Young

Don't overlook the old gods.
They make sense to the fisher,
Farmer, tapper, barber,
Hatchet-man, medium.
On Cheng Meng they devour
Boiled fowls, drain the brandy,
Spill ashes in the ricebowl.

Returning to my mother's house
I remember them. She believed
When she was young; and now
Although an old woman.
Under the Angsana a bomoh
Sets a shrine. A bride-to-be dies,
Longs for a groom and is married
To an infant perished.
We bring hardboiled eggs stained red
To honour his first birthday.
These spirits are easily appeased
For we can interpret their wants.
The crimson eggs rot and stink,
But we dare not throw them out.

Mother's Song

Beautiful man, milk teeth bared in a trap,
    Whose mouth curls in despair,
    She smiles at your face.

Beautiful man, twitching boy's shoulders
    Like many golden carp
    Swimming to her gaze.

Beautiful man, your white skin turns redder,
    Your slit eyes grow wide,
    Your chin's fuzzed with moth.

Beautiful man, fingers knifing, stab
    Or roll, winding up thoughts
    Like fine hair, like cloth.

Beautiful man, leaning back stock-still, now
    Bunched in fury, fishy,
    You play at the groom.

Beautiful man, crowsfeet walk your brow.
    Your head pulls as the tide
    Silvering the room.

Beautiful man, bitter, slipping her grasp.
    Like strong medicine, harsh tea,
    She swallows her doubts.

National Poem

Junta:
Phantom panther:
Black shadow
Rustling in the
Background. Sound
Of spiked boots
Tearing
A green field.
Green: colour
Of jungle
Fatigues: nature
Of jungle drums
Drumming
So loud
We cannot hear.

Visiting Malacca

Some one lives in the old house:
Gold-leaf carving adorns the doors.
Black wooden stairs still stand
And wind like arms of slender women
Leading to the upper floors.
It is as I remembered,
But not itself, not empty, clean.

Some one has scrubbed the sand-
Stone squares and turned them red.
The marble yard is stained with rain,
But it has not fallen into ruin.
Weeds have not seeded the roofs nor
Cracked flowered tiles grandfather
Brought, shining in crates from China.

Someone has saved the old house.
It is no longer dark with opium
Or with children running crowded
Through passageways. The well has been capped,
The moon-windows boarded.
Something of China remains,
Although ancestral family is gone.

I dream of the old house.
The dreams leak slowly like sap
Welling from a wound: I am losing
Ability to make myself at home.
Awake, hunting for lost cousins,
I have dreamed of ruined meaning,
And am glad to find none.

Returning to the Missionary School

Will the dull bell ring? The cracked
Nun in the tower strikes and strikes.
Down in the tropical compound
Where red-lipped hibiscus stick
Thick pistils in the watery air,
The town's daughters say their prayers.

A country of lessons: they stand
Crocodile-line on a playing field,
While, like starched wash drying.
At noon the Angelus peals
Downwards in billows
Of damp pinafores.

An old barren woman taught
Music to school girls then, beating
A down-beat with a ruler.
I walk backwards, measuring
How a tuneless tune can span
So many singing children.

Simple natives believe in
Breastless women stuffed with God,
Instructing monotone of
Sing-song behind walls glass-jagged.
What's sacred must be possessed
Beneath white vestal dress.

Alone, in mid-life, I return
To the parochial school, listen
For that loud clamour in
The sky — and hear children's jargon,
The lolling bell, clearly
Clap desire and old irony.

I Remember

I remember clearly child and sea.
With time, both have grown surer.
When, once, listening to water,
She thought to remember the sea,
Precise to smell, the grain
Of shore and gathering wave,
Mind worked furious with the grave
Attempt. All senses strained
To hold steady the blue motion
Looked at.
                    Where she had been
Then, there is no recognition.
I see her, now, the scene of a scene,
Planted eminent as the sky,
As sea she had enclosed in eye.

Song of an Old Malayan

Will you sell me, also, down the river
of nationalism, my sometime brother,
who know your accent, can speak your poetry?
Your family and mine, croaking, drank from the same well.
Now you are grown rich. Your sisters swell
with rank, buying hand-cut chandeliers
from Bohemia. Your wife *tak nampak saya,**
we who'd read from the same books. Her vision
of the future sparkles as purity.
Shall I sink silently to the stream's muddy bottom
while gold flecks rise to your hands like scum?
But you need me, my brother. How else
to find thorn of martyrdom,
rose of the east, your history's self?

*doesn't see me

No Man's Grove

Crossing the China Sea, we see
Other sailors, knee-deep in padi,
Transformed by the land's rolling green.
We cannot enter their dream.

The sea brings us all to jungle,
Native, unclaimed, rooted, and tangled
On salt like one giant tree.

We spring straight from sea-wave. We see
But do not see grey netted pliants
Shutting out the sun. Where sea and plant
Twine, mammoth croakers crawl on tidal zone.

Some will live in the giant's shade, bend
To the rapidly rolling horizon.
I choose to walk between water and land.

DEDICATED TO CONFUCIUS PLAZA

Dedicated to Confucius Plaza

I live in a small house
On top of fifty other houses.
Every morning I face the East River
Where the air is cold as
On Tung Shen Mountains.
The mountains are made of loess
Brought down by the Yang-tze.
The city is a mountain
Also, made of Asia,
Europe and Africa.
They call it America.
Every morning I practice *li*,
Perform my wifely duties,
Watch colour television,
And eat pop, crackle, snap.
It is not hard to be
An Asian-American Chinee.

Apartment B

We hear the others moving
Night after night. One sneezes,
Another answers, a phone rings,
But we do not wish to know
How they live. Having them so close
Is painful enough. We do not want
To hear them speak: only hear
Their inaudible voices,
Like their music and company,
Contained in boxes; hear only
Evening sounds of barks and sirens
To remind us we are human.
Any other speech may break
The bond which keeps us apart.

To Li Po

I read you in a stranger's tongue,
Brother whose eyes were slanted also.
But you never left to live among
Foreign devils. Seeing the rice you ate grow
In your own backyard, you stayed on narrow
Village paths. Only your mind travelled
Easily: east, north, south, and west
Compassed in observation of field
And family. All men were guests
To one who knew traditions, the best
Of race. Country man, you believed to be Chinese
No more than a condition of human history.
Yet I cannot speak your tongue with ease,
No longer from China. Your stories
Stir griefs of dispersion and find
Me in simplicity of kin.

Translation from Other Languages

Going through the city across traffic
Lights, blinding sun, seeking the cool shadow
Of buildings, I look for the man I love.
He is learning another language.
His mother braids her hair and veils her face.
He is learning to forget her.
He has crossed oceans and returned
To the noise of bulldozers and cars.
Conversing on new hills and clearings,
How foreign he has grown away
From jungle and sea-breeze! A scholar,
A gentleman, history will claim him.
He flourishes on the pavements,
Renewed in beauty of translation.

Modern Secrets

Last night I dreamt in Chinese.
Eating Yankee shredded wheat
I said it in English
To a friend who answered
In monosyllables:
All of which I understood.

The dream shrank to its fiction.
I had understood its end
Many years ago. The sallow child
Ate rice from its ricebowl
And hides still in the cupboard
With the china and tea-leaves.

Unforgiven

She knows I live here
In my house in Geylang.
Who would believe she belonged
Once, nested in my womb?
I write, It is so hot,
I pray for rain, for fortune.
My bad luck haunts her.
From the white land she posts
Green bundles, her filial remorse.
My unsleeping eye
Waits for her arrival.
Will she come out of the sky
Into my lap? Or stay there,
Where drifting ice will dome
Her cold, silent home?

The Windscreen's Speckled View

I
It is the usual once again.
We have rehearsed it
a dozen times or more.
Still we are never prepared
for the real thing,
for the real mother
to really die, for some real
figure in our real lives
no matter how far,
how lost, how never ours,
to slip away before we'd known
we'd never known them.
Reflections of losses:
twice absences.
A mute violence
with no mark unless
we cut ourselves,
no hurt except in
our shamefaced frenzy:
echo of a cry never made:
grief for a woman
who was once our mother.

II
Fifteen years later, I am returning
to watch you die. Now I am the woman
waiting for your event, coming with only
what I can afford — snaps of your grandson,
my sharp unhappy face to share the air
at point zero. No missionary,
I offer no after-life — bare fact
of family being your only blessing.

Only the mind's rich ironies persist
in relevance, through betrayals,
non sequitors, repeated nothings. So
cradled in Business' blue-checked upholstery,
sun-dashed American jagged land
below, I feel my life driven on these
unnatural winds, and feel my time
powered to the pitch in this flight from life
to death, from your dying to my release
on the borders of my mortality.

III

Drawing nearer to you, rounding
the figure, yet I am losing the race.
You are receding into fiction so fast:
a blurry snap of a fidgety child,
a succession of multiple distortions.
Is reality the vibrations
between wings, past action and present being,
the woman there and this woman here?
I imagine you breathing still,
pallor of suspension between
resisted life, resisted death
while, uplifted on metal struts,
I fly in the face of your transfiguration.

IV

Soon to be a ghost you tilt,
dragging oxygen mask i-v wires,
on the para-zone. Great clanging,
tumults charge into my eyes.

I have never loved you enough,
resenting your life's mistakes —
weedy self-love, blooming late,
rotting into religion, faked

salvation; suspecting you have
left them all to me. Opened,
unblinking, these brain scans lull,
scarcely hover, like wings beaten

before settling. You are changing
into the sing of your defeat,
while I am amazed by tears,
ungrateful even for this gift.

V
The windscreen's speckled view —
black, oily water quivering soundlessly under dull
october clouds; a wide low
roof, faintly Japanese.
No one in sight at 3 p.m.
Workmen, joggers, mothers and children, lovers
vanished from the slippery surface
into which chewing gum wads, candy wrappers,
cigarette butts have disappeared.
From the left open window
green-handed mallards kick greedily
in rich brown splashes.
Last winter's black stray
sniffs the garbage pails. No flies swarm in this mild air.
Yellow face in sideview mirror
looks at herself between deaths — oil
of fatigue smeared clumsily on
a face of blown autumn:
one would think she is bored of the company she keeps —
turgid nineteenth century characters
so long unburied they have dried
in the creases of her eyelids.
But a puff of crematorium smoke arouses her,
oily, brief in the noon tropics:
mother, smoking, in final blaze.
And only her charred fragments —
large shards of skull, long leg bones — were identifiable.
These asiatic reveries disturb some wavering sense:
not like those vigorous ducks paddling for dear life,
but as apparitions, crossing
between unwashed windscreen
and some suburban park.

Identity No Longer

Identity no longer carried in a card,
her passport declares 'dare to believe'.
Citizenness of the world, she approaches the Republic
of feeling.
   But who would credit her claims
knowing how the world fails most applicants
even as she whispers to spirit-lovers (of
all shades and persuasions: gruesome Eliot
finally a dirty old man, and ponderous Pound
peeing among her pages, Willy
whisking his Irish horn-pipe
and stern J.V. calling her schoolmasterly to task)
the line for the exit shuffles off and she,
caught short, between, waves only her papers.

Cross-Cultural Exchange
(Singapore 1986)

The pink-and-glossy man wants the little chap
to bring back the water glasses. He settles
on the platform and calls for questions. The plain jane
from the Ministry of Culture wants to know
how to be modern without becoming Ike and Tina
Turner. Her chinese convent voice is constantly
apologizing on the edge of rudeness.
We don't have a national culture, she complains,
nervously eying the Aussies and Kiwis
and the jolly-brown woman from Papua New Guinea.
We have value-added industries, central
provident fund, cheap taxis, housing
development board, glass hotel and,
of course, the people's action party.
But we don't have a national culture.
How to make one without Ike and Tina Turner?
The pink-and-glossy man sits up smacking his lips.
It's just the kind of question he relishes.
You must remember, he begins, in the beginning
was the word. You people speak English
very well, it shows how civilized you are
and that you are ready for a national culture.
Second, he goes on, divinity is in the air,
and is more present now airconditioning
has made Singapore tolerable ha ha.
Third, we in New Zealand have seen it all:
landfall, mountains, lakes, hotsprings, native trouble,
sheep, an angry god. You can learn from us.
As we can learn from you. Next question?

Chinese in Academia

Away from the streaky windows'
venetian blinds, the sun pours
from cold sky on beaten grass. Shadows
move past afternoon. I walk down
and up the speckled tile floor.
Cinderblocks glisten bluish-bright
under flourescent banks. There will
always be a person staying till
the last for a two-hour exam.
The wall-clock drips its seconds. She
is pink-cheeked and wants an A for
the accounting test. She doesn't know
I am twenty years older,
that shadows have moved past noon.
It is quiet here but not silent.
The blushing bulbs hiss like bees
feeding their queen. I am queen of fluorescent
lighting. Shoes scuff. Outside the corridor
is full of vanishing people.
They've been tested and have come through.
I have picked up two pens, two broken pencils,
a stack of squared sheets on which I write...
My life is a square of others' tests.
She bends over the computer paper,
soft stomach creased above dungarees.

I am reminded of myself, young girl
facing a two-hour exam, locking
thighs against the wish to urinate
while my pen scratches a future.
History is crammed with exam fever.
I look at the young woman fated
to make her fortune. I am afraid
I have studied far too long,
the day of reckoning is here and
I know nothing. Knowledge is security.
Frightened, I wait for the examiner.
I know only my life will always be
what it is, powerless, ignorant.
There will always be exams
I cannot pass. Chinese mandarins
learned of universal failure,
and I am learning that well, bent
over my watch, proctoring shadows
walking down and down the academic lawns.

Lament

I have been faithful
To you, my language,
Language of my dreams,
My sex, my laughter, my curses.
How often have I
Stumbled, catching you
Short when you should be
Free, snagging on curves,
Till fools have called me
Fool. How often have you
Betrayed me, faithless!
Disowned me — a woman
You could never marry,
Whom you have tired
Of long ago.

I have been faithful
Only to you,
My language. I choose you
Before country,
Before what eyes see,
Mouth, full-hearted, taste.
I choose you before
Lover and husband,
Yes, if need be,
Before child in arms,
Before history and all
It makes, belonging,
Rest in the soil,
Although everyone knows

You are not mine.
They wink knowingly
At my stupidity —
I, stranger, foreigner,
Claiming rights to
What I have no right —
Sacrifice, tongue
Broken by fear.

Night Perspective

A world here? Why not. The night
Will cast perspectives,
The low red moon persist,
Vagrant, historical.
We do not choose the light which shows
The street before us, or the street
Where tall ramshackled houses sit
Becalmed in a dim refraction.
We walk, lit by a round moon
On slow ascent, scenting
Forsythias we do not choose to note:
Slight, damp evocation that soon,
Perhaps, we cannot choose to forget.
Here the pavement veers sharp left.
The small-town topography
Plunges into confusion.
Our attention is claimed by grey snow,
A corner, the railroad horizon
Distorted by timber, made forlorn
By spacings of light, by desertion.
The world claims. Its geography
Gives us the shapes we have this night.

Thoughts from Abroad

Late through October the leaves change colour.
The season has been around so long most
Do not see it go to winter.
From our window-height we watch the year close
In the trees. About us, the rural land
Reflects the sunlight. Far away,
Unglimpsed, the Atlantic makes a band
Of mirrors for Massachusetts. Today,
The scene is exulting: to air and light
Houses, trees and highways seem sensible
Moment to moment; till we can quite
Imagine this world invisible
As instinct on the flood for home
From which all exiled landscapes come.

Winter Approaching

In such times, autumn seems to surprise
Anew with power to decay;
With various harvests yet to come, to die,
Decay, and grow, a seasonal constant.
Flame and ruin once again will seize
The summer solid-seeming landscape; the day
Begin with birds low flying on currents
West and south. In a moment, the bent
Of wide sky shifts from blue to grey.

Indecisive weather such as this
Displays the many autumnal ways
Of dying; while we, watching, wonder where
The show of life leaves off and world's air
Sinks down to winter death, if death it is.

New England

Fall let loose a blaze
into blue windy days;
is slush now where we go
in air cold with coming snow.

See how through wet woods
squirrels skitter. Broods
of jays show off wing
in and out of tangled twigs.

No clarifying yellow
here. Late fall is grey
and bright, a colour
for a still-life day
imaginable
as bliss, and sensible.

Character-Sketch

Stooped, six-foot and a half,
Bad teeth, age-freckled
Wrists neatly cuffed,
Mister Varley lives
In a large wood home.
Oriental carpets
Keep the feet warm.
Branches of bitter-sweet
Curve in a jar.
No bureau, high bed,
Mobiles of prisms,
Sea-shells, intrude.
Each shapes a clean space
For living pared
Down to beauty.

In Learning We Suffer Death

In learning we suffer death: the old man,
Rising, hobbling from pit to crossroads,
Defies all signs of pure intention.
"Nothing can save you!" he cries, and we
Pull from his influence. It was no dream
For young girls, but I was twenty-four.
Mornings I woke to the light of meaning,
Sprinted across railroad tracks, shortcut
To the glassy campus, brittle, gifted
By Usden, Schwartz, Goldberg, and Neumann,
Old men tottering in high places;
Saw narrow faces, mean November slits
Festering among tangerine maples,
Acid browns and spots in ashy birches
Pulling away in zero weather.
My old teacher cried, "Before life, death!"
And I read the books, enduring
"The mundane madness," drift of a
Continent toward green-berried winter.

Simple Simon or the Suicide

He never arrived on time.
Authorities sent the body
In to order the discovery
Of death. Thus he submitted, poor Simon,
To the indignity of the nude,
The cold gliding cut and probe.
In admiration amateurs groped
At the treasures fitted within: blood
Ruby fresh, lungs uncorroded
By hateful living. Jewelled
Kidneys, tight unblemished heart,
All these he kept as if to start
Someplace anew. In such unwarranted death,
Was sewn, whole, dispatched to earth.

Anna's Faith

A foot of fresh snow arrived today,
a foot of white with no grey or yellow
in it. You would have been eighty today.
Other birthdays rejoice this morning.

Some years brought blue crocus,
fisted hyacinths, narcissi early forming.
Today brought snow you would have murmured
at. Your home was musty, clean, smelling

of soap chips, like you after years of rinsing.
Catholic, bent small and propped on pillows,
a baby labouring for breath, you viewed
the park's grey lichen without a shadow

of irony, pressing your childless palm, light
as a page, on my sleeve. One would want to pretend
for you more love than one had; to be good outside
one's self, condescension at your pliant faith

in weak tea and crochet squares muted through
your dying to something else, perhaps,
better; for once, late in the evening,
kissing the papery cheek goodbye, true.

American Driving

Looked up yesterday, saw
I was the only woman around,
Strapped in my maroon Volvo
Station, drifting down

At fifty-five miles per hour.
Earth's landscape braced, spun,
Myself headed to interior,
Slowly round a wintry sun.

Today, in caucasian countryside,
I race trees like heads bristling
With beauty's subtle shadowed light,
Topple hilly faces. Still,

In Aladdin's garden
With weightless hemlocks and rosy
Stone, I float on my magic wagon.
I want to pull, dizzily,

Into a break-down lane, to stop
And look at life. The car keeps moving,
It snarls in its own top
Wind. My mother's hand is reaching

From fat autumn clouds. "Where
Are you going? Who are you?"
She moans through windowed glare.
But I drive on, going too

Fast. If I don't make an error
Or turn to a dead-end narrow
Road, I drive forever.
Or, at least, until tomorrow.

The Mind of the Beholder

Beauty is in the mind of the beholder.
The tree is maple, showing through October
A fury of colour.
                Thousands register,
Planted by the highway like blue sky,
The scene as seen in memory.

Alone on the Parkway driving with the stream,
I see it briefly, emblem, American dream,
Blanketing little white towns and houses
Shingled with golden leaves. Lawn mowers
And bicycles left in its shade discern
Our mood and rust through the season.
New smoke carries the bitter scent of country,
Reminding of lavender, herbs, elm-tree,
Wondrous details townspeople think
We should want. The mind is loaded to the brink
Of tenderness.
                Seeing a maple reflect
Sunset, we remember nature and regret
Its absence; believe absence is beauty.

A LIFE OF IMAGINATION

In Praise of a Master

We thought when first we saw him,
It was cold which made him colder
Than he was. Against the wind
He had set his smile. Behind
His back, the weight of winter
Fell on stones and frozen birds.

The seasons will not thaw him,
Who had lived to know his portion
Of men's praise. What other gaze
Than indifference could face
That self-most steadfast motion
Sought and lost again in words?

Master in his craft, he'd come
To finished form, perceived
What words may give. He professed
In Silence self the rest:
What must be unconceived,
Speechless, the remainder

Of all remaining; final, dumb,
And shaping bell of self. Human
And frail, with woe and love no less
Than with what's passionless
He lived; living, was what man,
Making, his self may master.

reincarnation
(for jv cunningham)

sitting alone with coffee i startle
myself thinking of another teacher
nursing his cup through afternoons
alone in silent rumination
even the black carpenter ant has more
in mind as it scuttles to potted
shiny hibiscus while i ponder air
in the leafy cascade from a second
storey balcony knowing an old teacher
crumbling in a compact clay breathes
in my woman's body to refresh his cup

The Will

There is a will resisting resistance; we inhabit
Those spaces given up by ghosts we disinherit.

On Water

Water unconfined
Looks for boundaries.
If finding none,
Sinks to larger ground.
Of this I'm certain:
Any lake or pond
Or river rises
Because of stone,
Crack, and mountain.

All life, some said,
Is water. Yet contained,
It can be constant.
Only images reflected
Shift, warp, and blur
With air or sediment
Stirred. Water remains,
Although not the same
As was a moment past.

All things are repeated
In themselves. No use
To deny thus
By thinking on water.

Not One Beauty

No, there is not one
Beauty which alone
Satisfies mind
And heart. Into a stone
You'll dream, blind
By Medusa's rage.
Past old age,
Woman, you will find
In your single cage,
Dissolution's lust
Yet corrupts the dust.

To What Ends?

Poetry
asks understanding.
Its sign, compression,
acknowledges to conceal:
widening centric motions
of a swimmer floundering,
striking out for shore
or horizon, a sign
insistent on survival,
breaking the bottomless
surface of ocean.

Credo: 1

"True and false, they are the same," he says:
A voice resonating in the ear,
Substantial as the body
Distanced at line's end, in another place.
Now it is silent, I am freshly
Disturbed. If there is no distinction true,
The mirror in which I have seen clearly
Myself may itself be flawed. So, too,
In walking our own sure space,
Eyes looking out at passers-by,
Gazing at fragile singularity,
See everywhere a mirage, distraction.
All we can know with least destruction
Is self, in the little while, here.

Credo: 2

There should be priests for those who need to pray.
When, for instance, walking with crowds or friends,
Something seizes up, coughs out the day,
And we stand startled, having nothing to say
But saying still, so caught in the ordinary
Lie, there should be absolution, some ends
Kinder than laughter cracking on a cry,
Or faces which fugitively
Search a mirror for signs and cure.
Well-worn demons catch upon our elbows,
While we who cannot believe have no place
Of sanctuary, nor, even if we chose,
Any forgiveness as would secure
Blessings and illuminate our days.

The Look Turned Inwards

Perhaps the only
Certain gaze. Except,
If, when looking out,
One is encountered
By blank presences
Of stone, trees,
Or plain assertions
Which things make, table
Or door, for example.
Or when crossing the room
You come across a cat
And exchange each
A suspicious stare.

A Life of Imagination

Details got in the way:
A sinus congestion,
Waking flushed in the night,
Dreading the family disease.
Who would have thought he
Could so wonderfully
Concentrate his mind
On form? Pressing for
That honied sweetness
Which leaves upon the tongue
Its aftertaste and cloys
In time, he possessed it
In vision and called forth
Immaculate yearning.
Dreaming of a bridal chamber,
He burned in a pure
Fever, descrying lovers
In sensual embrace;
Limbs entwining, face pressed to face
Classically, their passions wrought
By his longing. So dreading
In mind, his poetry grew
Whole, packed, slow-moving
Towards time he would not live.

On Reading Coleridge's poem

"Alone on a wide wide sea!" he wrote;
And we, reading this, wonder if he'd known
What it was all about. How then could he
With this passion live, frightening
Every stranger, the strange old sea-dog?
Or else made passionate monologue,
Out of harm's way, harmless, trusting
To construct passing and indestructible,
Word upon word, felicity?
Remembering too, the wished-for return,
The forgiving priest, the willing pilot,
The throng by the harbour, curious, appalled —
We could hope this was true; but know here
Like the passing stranger, only pity, fear.

Imagine

Imagine —
a sheet of glass
reflecting nothing
but itself.

No image —
all surface
a pure depth.

Still —
words are significations
of things other than.

All poetry
necessarily
begins with a lie.

Thoughts on a Cezanne Still-Life

Transform deep to depth, dazzle to clarity.
Arrest movement to gesture, time to moment;
Turning neither left nor right, but standing still,
To make stillness, and stillness a vocation;
Selecting of the world's pieces, one:
A beauty to set on a shelf, to gather
From the quiet air a fine film of dust,
A form, enclosed, of grains falling
Noiselessly along a shaft of bright sun.
Or, imagine a sheet of glass reflecting
Nothing but itself. No image, all surface
A pure depth: the creature material
Poised in solitariness, at once
Ineffable and bright, blinded as terror.

No Alarms

Tonight the mind will not let go.
Poisoned by the day's slow envy
Of those not more talented, I grow
Sad and look for poetry.

The husband beneath my arm labours
Downhill like a broken motor.
Sleep knocks him senseless; his body
Stretched beside, I feel, is almost me.

Through this crack of distance from the bed,
I sharpen pencil, light a cigarette,
Recall the day past, hoping for insight,
Image to make life certain. Tonight,

Pausing at tasks I search for the other.
Waiting for attention year after year,
Has she packed off finally, disappeared?
Drowned in this drowsiness I suffer

Nothing, see nothing waiting on the page,
No alarms, no passions, no order, no rage.

To Marianne Moore

Where is the toad?
In the garden we
Did not build,
Deciding against
Stories of the mind
While dying
Like everyone else.
Where is the island?
Sailing in the night
Moonwards.
We have shut
Imaginary doors
Decisively.
The door to the mind
Does not exist
But admits one only.
Here is our denial,
Real.
Like anything else,
We deny it.

Science-Fiction

I dreamed a science-fiction movie:
A giant thing, half-bird, half-octopus,
With beak to tear and flapping wings
Gauzy as tissue drifting in the air
That lifted its monstrous weight rapidly.
It was a mother screeching for its babe,
Loathsome, propelled by love and loss;
The baby, caught by human curiosity.
The natural process of the mind,
Studying, saw the off-spring wrinkle, shrink,
Black as a scrap of chicken skin,
To its damaged foetus.
                        And as
The mother-creature burst into the dream,
We ran, I the most fearful,
The first to crawl beneath a space,
Then, chased out to the open a breathless time,
Woke, out of breath, remembering my sins.

On Hearing a Woman Poet read

She wears her face plainly on her face,
Reading her words for all to see.
Skin tugged over jaw, over space
Taut as a drum and scraped raw on cheek;
Not fine translucence but spotted,
Blotched by feeling or pain. We gaze
Into eyes opaque, clotted
By vision, and read in her irises
Certain texts we may have written also.
On thorny legs she reads. Poetry is...
Is woman's plant, stellar
Brilliance, body opening in kiss
Of welcome.
                    Are you our sister whose words
Awaken in rooms of strangers to know
Yourself? A long-legged bird
Startled by sound, you clear air, show
Flight, before falling again
To the close of your poem, to your pain.

The Painter, Munch

The painter caught the dumb mouth,
Fixed wide, in a man out walking
Down a road. One moment past,
He was pleasantly musing
With the sun shining south
Behind him. Air and hills
Are drawn together
In blue and green paste
When the painted mouth is stilled.
Afflicted by knottier
Pigment, the eye, off-guard,
Suffers and goes mad,
In *rigor mortis*.

The Painter

He always liked mirrors,
Painted them blue, yellow, green,
With glitter, panache, with sheen,
Like liquid turning to ice,
A cold slick of something
Substantial and reflecting.
He put corners on them,
And frames. Squares and rectangles,
His mirrors were windows.
Standing to one side, on an angle
Of vision, he glimpsed numerous
Folds of the world, unseen
Himself. He painted nothing
But mirrors and filled his house
With reflecting canvas.
He could not step through them.

Piano-Player

The scales she practices are sharp and clear;
It was so easy to learn, plucking
At will melody to being. Her seven years
Have not guessed at this joyous ringing
Herself created. Listen, eyes say,
It is I who am playing the music
Unheard till I struck the keys. Gay
Run the notes, precise the child's jig:
Garden drawn with flowers, melons, birds;
A gate which shuts tight at her word.

Song grown simple, she rehearses
Another, grand, sombre, hesitating
At tune. How wavering comes that burst
To the mother at the doorway listening,
Though her child plays, and only years have passed,
Only she has played on ivory keys.
Music was made, hung in the moment, cast
Out. She tries a different piece
Her fingers cannot win. Complexity
Is the music she desires. To be

Always one note behind the wonderful;
To break the pure board for what still
Is hidden, for shadows in the pool
Of light reflecting sound; to fill
The vibrating room; leave, return, find
The player sitting by the instrument
Closing her eyes. Not music but a kind
Of music waiting to be learned.
Thirty years have not readied her for
The particular, sense unshut, sorrow.

An Immigrant Looks at Whitman

Something wonderful and different
Might turn to memorialize
The wide water of his death.
Second death. There are earthquakes
Daily. Bombs go off and little-
Known shop-girls are blown away,
Chin off, legs off at the knee.

The major prophets gazing upwards
Saw celestial maze, dark redoubts,
Not the saw-whet owl or long
Purples deep in marshes.
But, for you, bring golden pheasant,
Goldenrod, my Asia, my America.
I fish in the Great Lakes inwards,
Forsaking gods for leeches and wild pansy.

The Radio

The voice I hear from a radio
Is neither black nor plastic.
Blowing through the stale
Room, it wears emotion
On silky sleeves and slinks
Across the floor: a woman
Singing like the natural
Nightingale comforting
A forgotten Chinese emperor
With memory of easy living.

Better than city moonlight,
Her nocturnal song sweeps
My narrow bed, shows poor
Chairs and tables, broken things
Which can't be helped. Twenty
Floors above ground level,
From the small black box, piano,
Basses, flutes and trumpets leap,
Escort her, primma donna,
Through the rich glowing door.

I Defy You

I defy you Wallace Stevens
to prove 'the exquisite truth.'
Your thirteen blackbirds rolled in one
continuous seamless world
bob in and out of my world
as do the black men and women
in Durban who skitter
on my tv screen. There is something else
than mere vision, mere imagination,
fat man of language. Something
than words and quiet time and cold mind,
although you have emptied your pockets
and peeked over the horizon of our desires
and turned back preferring your onanistic treasures.
The young Cambodian whose father drowned
in monsoon ocean knows
his sister's raped eyes are truth;
the hungry and dead are his 'exquisite truth,'
and you an American fiction.

THE ELEMENTS

Land-Turtle

A land-turtle: the fine gold tracery
He drags about, webbing his green belly,
And turns to every giant child and dog
A hard back like a mud-splashed chip of log.
Crawling to no place particular, taking
His time, to his particular undeflecting
Desire. And if you must meddle with his
Travels, the bright little face disappears
In comic alarm; some say modestly,
Though I have thought I had caught in his button eyes
A dismissal too uncomfortably like contempt.

Crocodile

Terribly afraid, keeping under water,
The small muscular crocodile drifts
Close to the town. Her lidless eyes waver
In the flow. Green leaves pass by her mouth
Like fishes; they too are native, going down
To sea. Jaws, empty and ravenous,
Glide in brown water, turning up crowns
Of weed, mud, rusty cans. An old tire
Springs from its bed like a corpse escaping:
She smells the warm body of a bather
Singing to the light. Oh what is the timing
Of this place with her hunger, the swimmer
With her fate? The drowned log rises with a sensation
Of falling and consumes the flesh, its passion.

Bat

I wake in an instant,
Arms, legs, askew in bed
Like a bat, spread four-limbed
Outstretching, flattened to go.
Tissues of nerve web the wing-span
And connect it to my brain.
Images swoop like the shadows
Thrown as it wheels about
Flanged and fanged; a silhouette
Crooked as a primitive cut-out,
Banging on the mental screen.
I have trapped it in my dream.
Mewing, it scrabbles to be let out.
I wake in an instant, afraid.

Whale

Underwater, the grey,
hulking sperm whale grunts,
bites the rope hooked in his lung.
The wise and shining head turns
in foam; his eyes, too small,
blurs with pain. Then bloody water
spouts and sprays the brave
fishermen of the Azores.

Shell

I found a mollusc high
In Massachusetts mountain
Under a hemlock tree.
Its ridges were packed
With dirt curiously.
Ancient, crustacean, a sign
Pointing the road to sea
For watchful travellers —
The note I stumbled on
Was not for saunterers
Like me. I should have left
It there for someone else,
But brought it back instead —
My shell of no particular beauty.

The Elements

I fall asleep when I meet you,
The hapless sleep of infants
Or animals or violent sleep
Of winter when life goes under
Radically: so quiet, hearing
Order in the times, forfeiting
Leaf stir and wood shadows
To find again stone scraping against root
And earth, water, air.
Unnatural semblance of sleep!
When all around the world shakes off
Foliage and embraces darkness.
You are my great killing winter.
I fall asleep in the elements.

After Fall-Out

What will become of us?
Our nerve fails with each year;
It's not as in the past.

Old powers venemous
War on. Our children fear,
What will become of us?

When once the seasons cast
Fresh flowers, birds appear:
It's not as in the past.

The bare earth's winds will gust
On cities, suns will sear.
What will become of us?

Our own creation's dust
Extinguishes us here.
It's not as in the past.

Our first vision's trust
Is shattered, that mirror clear.
What will become of us?
It's not as in the past.

Shells

Home in Asia a sad salesman
Closing business in a less than deluxe
Hotel showed his wares: Midnight in Paris
Perfumes in jars small as my thumb, palm fans
Painted with hula girls and palm trees,
Faded batik lengths — all for a few bucks.

And gaudy shells — enormous whorls
From which the sea ran out, heavy
Suits for isolated tribes now dead;
These spirals, combs, ridged humps their only souls
Remaining. Dark mottled, lustred lead,
They were lovely, fished from Sabah sea,

Jewels of water. I held a smooth
And rosy conch designed in stipples,
Pearly bands not pink nor any color
Mixed by mind. As if a spirit had roofed
Independently the merest paint for
Ocean light and weightless ripples.

Full of despair he brought a spider
Shape, energy cased in spiny lime:
A fort with prongs and spikes advancing there
Through liquid silence! Out of water,
Ferocity lost its face, became the care
Of maids to dust, collectors's item.

Paid and bore both home, dead trappings
Of beauty which should have best been left
Alone, alive in bottom ground, unseen
By fisher or diver. Trawled by strings
Of human-kind, these ancient homes gleam
Abandoned to light and placeless; bereft.

The peddler shut his shop, hotel
Ran down. Permanent is the theft
Of beauty. Day by day, dragging
The world for possession, symbol, shell,
Amulet to keep as if a real thing
With life, where none or little life is left.

Another Spring

My life in everything but one is rich.
My students grown and young come running, hey teach,
Teacher, buenos dias. Adios amigos,
We say in leaving, children all and hosts
To early summer. Now tulips drop,
Peach petals tear, disclosing foetal crop.
The vine is trained, stays green and even
For nine months of the city's season.
Twenty kinds of grass flower in the patch.
I weed carefully. Overwhelmed by such
Luxury, there is no time, no time
For what is necessary; for answers,
For questions. The winter skin burns, yields
Tender, stem-yellow, for another
Spring and lying fallow in the fields.

In Defence of the Crooked

In nature nothing is simple.
Therefore, I make no simple response,
Not being straightforward.
Crooked, bent as a bonze,

I am bowed, tangled; worse,
Not seeing straight, but hinged
And glassy-eyed, to squint in light.
My body is out of synch.

Mouth dragged down to the side;
Breast lumpier than the other.
One rib bone curves high and hangs
To the west. My teeth stagger

To catch on celery strings
And tongue. Nervous, I stutter.
The last toe and companion curl
Like callouses. I bowl into gutters.

Therefore, I don't trust straight things:
Arrows which hit their mark; humans
Who sit up and stick their bellies in;
Direct propositions with no room

For misunderstanding. My answer
Is twisted, clarified by a lie
To praise the barbed plant, to exhort
Uncertain humanity.

August Heat

The August heat breeds unseemly
Thoughts, images like crickets mating
In the sun, drawn by sense, vibrating,
Crowding in the throat and belly.

What a nuisance is this lust
Lying like an assassin in the dark,
Silent, intent, and the park
A sudden wilderness thick with musk.

The threat of falling to the knife
Beats in my heart as I slowly walk
This afternoon, this heat, till stalks
Of love grown over brush and drive

Me to the open empty page.
The impulse of summer is pure
Cascading water, endures
Crashing against roof or fence or cage,

Falls as a flood as though to wash
Away foundations, force
Casements down and with hoarse
Guttural voice our lives unleash.

A catbird creaks from a hidden leaf.
Exhausted, the iridescent
Dragon-flies blur, descend.
We look for cover, lover and thief.

Summer Bugs

On a blue morning the golden bugs zip
Like metal wires to the sun; their dance
Approaching, zagging, meeting, antennae tipped
For the search, a secret quiver, lance.

I watch them in the open hollow
Between house and woods plunge into air.
Katydids clinging to the tulip trees blow
And rasp. I am bitten in my lair

By bugs; see long-legged spider daddies
Wobble like old men to the table.
Pale green sandflies hop in bed, half-tease,
Half-jaws, clipping summer flesh. Sable

Furred mites burrow in yellow stems;
Colonies of white flies have massed on
The drooping palm. Every hour the sleazy hum
Of munching, sucking, mating. I am gone

To sleep, sick as a potted plant chewed
By golden bugs hurtling in my blood.

At the Pool

The polar air rolled in last night;
We pulled tattered blankets from their store.
How sticky hot all last week was, and bright
With long summer's langorous desires.

By noon the children had jumped into the pool.
Blue faces drifted under water
Like swamps of lotus or as schools of fools
Drowned in their images and lit by fires

From the shifting glass, eyes glazed
By the self-undulation of the wave.
Heat and water will turn docile babies crazed,
And in the mobile element upheld

Scores swooped, boogied, somersaulted, flew.
I felt my thickening body brave
Beside their agile senses: that I could view
The rapt child-sensuous play and not be sad!

Brinjal

Fragrant brinjal, purple hazed or
sheen of amethyst; ovaloid female,
pendulous; as shoe polish slicked;
unevenly round, glowing moon's rump
smelling of colours; in farm's wet
morning — ordure of night soil; impenetrable
skin like first sex; shiny as spit,
as slippery; rubbery feel
jousting the palm: you remind
anything in nature is woman's
and man's (overflowing potency,
sultanate of suggestions by river flats),
tickles fancy, excites memory's
warm ooze — these water-smooth firm-toothed
veggies, names jingling like slave anklets
in rattan baskets heaped, abused
by kitchen women, slapped into newspaper wrappers
in the market this morning, fresh talents!

Panther

Lying by his sleeping side
the midnight panther stares
at me. Immobilized
she crouches. She has fed
full of something, the fullness
films her pupils. Listen,
sleeping sounds — the single crash
of a raindrop multiplied
against the shrill echoes of a country night
passing for silence —
reach the creature.
She is unmoveable
except for the wired force
in her wary head. Sharp-edged
ears, dense shiny nose,
alert, contemptuous, the head
is a bowl in which passions hiss
like acids and sulphurs.
But the bowl is a classic thing,
it does not move. So my classic
panther, sullen, female,
lies all night unmoving.

Cactus

Early one morning, hard at work,
I look up and see the office cactus.
Gone weeks without water, it has
Sprouted monstrously. Like an odd dark
Dream, this wrinkled flesh laced with pinky fuzz
And thorns, this complex growing in
Old pebbles and worn-out sand, in nothing
But a plastic pot, rises by the glass
Window and shines. How does it do it,
Thin as a pencil and upright carrying
A fat spiky head? All prickles, unaccomplishing
Blossom or seed, bearing itself as fruit.

The Gate

After the day's rage, the quiet:
the flower garden, the gate
ajar, the woman smoking
in slovenly solitude.
An attitude to adopt
almost naturally, as mood
suggested by moon and tide.
All else beyond: concrete condos,
tepid Singapore air, scorpions
in a city night. To follow
the natural contours of an
unnatural world, wondering.
Where is the stir by which we know
our own? Estranged yearning
falling almost naturally below
into shapes of garden, gate,
a woman alone smoking.
Again and again the grate
of anger in a glass-and-stone
night without moon's anchor,
without scent and tide's quiver.
How then to make of this quiet
after day's rage a human gate?

WOMEN'S DREAMS

Night Vision

Years later, I lie awake
In the deep enclosing heart of a household.
Years later than in a crib,
Floating among the white moon faces that beam and grasp.

Years later, flecking the eyes,
Faces like spheres wheeling, savouring my self.
Years later, I awaken to see
Dust falling in the dark, in the house.

Early Poem — 1

My dreams are
mixed with
poetry,
and my nights are
good nights.
Who knows when
gladness
becomes
the day, and
who cares,
anyway?

Early Poem — 2

Lovers most often
speak in poetry.
Both lie.
Words are
true only
to themselves,
as birds are neither
nesting tree nor sky,
but themselves
alone
their true soliloquy.

Dressing Room

As I dress
in front of
the mirror
I hear
gunshots,
dying dogs,
and remember
child crying
for a dead pup.
And somehow,
how easily
the ornaments of
gladness
are dislodged,
the mirror
showing itself
dusty
with spilt powder.

Child

Makes paper dolls from odds
And ends, furtively dresses
And furtively tears them.
She plays in lonely places;
Shade under trees, grass
By a silted lake in evening.
Her strained mute person shrinking
Through late afternoons
Or among early stars
Invites a cruelty: a
Stranger observing her
Tenderness, to slit the throat
And gag her dissonant joy.

Girl

Girl, pensive and chaste by your desk,
I recognize your lie
This morning raw with sunshine.
Your soaped and scrubbed self alone
Shines in the neat landscape; your eyes
Avoid the wavering breezes.
Critical, you spy
On our unkempt household,
The twitching nose upturning
A cache of poverty.

I love you, girl, who proudly tests
Your growing breasts,
Firming your body to the race;
The clear look that accuses
Our love and destruction, assuring
That when our round earth shrivels,
Your chaste mouth will smile and smile.

Speech

How shall we speak except
Of what we neither of us mean?
Speech which should lie silent
Falls like an ocean without sail.

The vacant space between
Never fills, for you turn vacant
When I come, come pleading,
Yet unable to ask; afraid
You will not understand,
Or, understanding, you cannot give.

Between is a gap I pretend not to know,
Because between you and I is nothing.
Speech, if it comes, can never tell of silence,
And our silences are now merely gaps.

Tell me, what have we lost,
Which cannot be said, which
Was there, and which no longer
Breathes in our silences?

If I were everything,
I would bury speech.
If I could, I would bury
What seems now lost and never found,
Whose absence is so largely present.

Shopping

I cannot praise you too little:
You are nothing much.
When I look around to gauge
With a computing eye
Each one, the computer-heart
Registers prices: dollars-
And-cents, plus-minus status
Taxation. In air-conditioned,
Music'd, lit, white supermarket,
Chattering with the coiffures,
I am an elegant starling
Coxcombing the alleys.

Stranger

Stranger, he,
picking his nose,
alarms.
Everyday slips
out of joint.
I suffer
tentativeness,
shying away
from a new
land breeze.
He, hunched in place,
Him self, bone and
touched flesh and
stubbles, teeth,
tongue within, whole.

Strange, afraid:
only this way I know.
Evening lurches;
I scuttle
Away, from.
My handhold, foothold,
wholeness, where?

Daphne

Because she could not outstrip the intent god,
She roots in constant flight and warp.
What mingled with the hardening sap
Or ran to harrow the freshening bud
With blight? Her glossy skin perhaps recoiled
To this bitter ruckle, that delicate rump
Transplanted to this bent of trunk.
Daphne, tasting the accommodating soil,
Knew then the consummating pain
Too soon for terror; would then have gladly lain,
Who now must be content to strip her green
To grieve a chase she would not lose nor win.

Queens

Scherezade in the night sits weaving
A net of stories to catch a king.
She weaves a rope to hold the world.
Her nets reach to horizons:
Before her, oceans and continents.
Skylines of towers lash her bright eyes;
Her lips' stain sets on the sunrise.
In daylight she moves regally,
Lightly, a butterfly launched on iridescent wing.

Take off your clothes, witchweaver Penelope,
Take your clothes off. The raucous lovers yell
Encouragement. Her bones sheathed within
The collected flesh are shuddering
With the shuttles. She spins a web
For an old man's death and a halter
For the greasy suitors; holds them there
Cunningly, the sly tongue tipped on the malicious grin.

Mannequins

Separated by glass, they beckon
Strangers from the sidewalk. Angular, thin;
Who love them are women. Reflection
Of Narcissus clothed in perfection,
A power invites us in their trance
Of shape; rosy, life-sized, and kin
To the alien whose strut and prance
Parade even in the sexual dance.
Image of surface, they are not filled
By others; mindless, breath cannot kill.
  In that shared conception, we
    Also study their perfect circuity.

To Jane

All night the thought of you disturbed me.
I couldn't swallow you, you were not credible,
Though you had hugged me, breasts and shoulders,
Saying I love you, I love you.
Why do we meet? I am confusion
In your presence. Among your big acts of supremacy,
How you love the world, I am guilty of compassion.
Now you will hate me for that sin.
I too want badly to be loved. How do you move
Your quick mouth, jump upon your heart,
Make faith which you give to all: Eat?
But I choke. It is love I cannot swallow.

Romance

There are some good women
You think you see through a room.
Their bodies exude a shining bloom,
Their heads roll on cushions
Like roses flushed and tangled.
But I have not met them.
So I stand at a distance,
Giving girls no encouragement
While they lie in sediment,
Bone-black and crow-jangled.

If I must marry someday
A woman like my aunts; say,
One with burnt skin, with ordinary
Breasts; who is gnarled, rancid, cursed:
I will punish her first!
She will cry and be sorry.

Winter Air

When in a dream, unsought, you came and touched,
I in such bliss refrained from waking;
So tasted, stayed the deep desired slaking
Of my lust; then sprang awake. It was too much
That was so little. Still will your ghost, my dear,
In morning familiar stalk the sphere
Of earth I walk in, shaken with winds and bare:
Inhabitant compassionless as air!

Children

It was hours in the woods they spent
Together, sneaking up to lodges
Where watch-dogs hummed a vicious sound.
Silent, they rounded a private bend
Of water, intent on geese drifting
By threes and fours, tucked from the wind.
A dead log flung to the pond was a raft,
A canoe. With the wind, a ship slipping.
When suddenly, crammed with cold air,
They retreated, subdued. Grown shy
And attentive, the awkward desire
All the long walk back kept them company,
Miserable. Two sullen friends
They said good-bye, unfriendly.

No One

No one, I thought, loved you as much as I,
Fearing to move abruptly or far
Lest I should lose you. And you, indulgent,
Had undertaken quiet lest I should cry.
No lovers were ever so loyal.
It was sure we knew each other well,
And what we knew we loved, forgetting
Neither the kiss goodnight nor morning.
So consoling, we made disconsolate
Each other; urged suddenly, to violate,
To shake the unshakeable-seeming firmament
And dance amuck, solitary among the stars.
Now gentled, each to each returned,
We ask, bewildered, where each had gone.

Song

It is not because I do not love
You wholly, that the heart does not pound
Nor head start, sprung by delight as move
Gulls glimpsed feeding on a rich mound.

Knowing no blessing flows from place,
Nor any fear which can kill or break,
Sounds we speak become ours. The face
So quietly lain is dear for its own sake.

The steadfast pace within we keep
Secured is our own life, not as
Sounds of life beleaguered, heard in sleep,
Pulsed fitfully in wars not past.

Danny Boy

The man upstairs is walking in his boots.
Naked, testicles swinging, he stomps on my ceiling
And wakes me. It is three in the morning.
I hear the boots knock corner to corner:
They are round-toed, black leather, Army and Navy
Surplus boots. He is a black leather Army man
Who stands by his window and waits
For the light to show in my room. I see
His obese shadow reflected in the glass.
Danny was a war baby; father
Gave him a German bullet when they met
And he tried to eat it immediately.
The man upstairs is practicing in his boots,
Left! Right! swearing Jesus! being Danny.

House-Hunting

We were looking for something.
For a year we searched the house,
Its closets, hallways, basement.
At times we heard its silent sigh
Or thought we smelt an odour
Like spring refreshing a corner.
  Impatient I began to smoke,
You took up writing and drinking
While we waited for it to show.
We gave up only the hope
Of finding it tomorrow.
  We will stalk it gradually,
We said, with great cunning
And with the patience of hunters
Laying winter traps for musk-rats;
We will sleep and wait for the traps
To catch.
          Or the animal
Does not live in the house now
Although we had bought it all:
Renovated brownstone, garden:
To polish stone mantels, open
Flues, and walk barefoot on pinewood.
Its high ceilings will out-wait us.
When we go, someone else will look for it.

Smoking

The whole house smells of my smoking.
You hate the stink, hate thinking
Of the germ which will devour me,
Your wife, and of your loss. And just
So, you hate me for your pain.
I will say I am sorry.
Smoke covers me: my skin is stained
Chinese yellow; my teeth are rust;
My hair is foul with ash.
In the linen chest the wash,
Neglected, grows grey with time.
The house cries for attention while
You sulk because the daffodils
Were not cut: lush precocious
Blooms now tumbling from their hills.
But I love their dying on stems,
Rank reminders of spring.

I Would Like

I would like to be happy as a servant:
Serve on committees, serve the community,
Serve the people, a government servant.
I would like to serve a family:
Clean house, polish flatware, arrange
Flowers, and fold away laundry,
Fluffed, lemon-scented, in symmetry.

Pure home-maker, hand-maiden, I,
A foot-stool, would serve you hand and foot.
Then would it be no effort to lie:
Sycophant, flatterer, lady,
Efficient at this as in the others.
My mouth would gape, sing arias,
Tongue, and burn black as widow's soot.

Seven Years

For seven years I have not met you
Again. Behind your desk you are writing
Another friendly letter addressed
To the people. You have grown older,
Of course; richer, of course; and better,
Like copper slowly burnished to tan.
At first you will not remember
Who had cried at your side, diminished
And sad. Your telephones are ringing
All day, and all night you will be sleeping
With the deep and easy mind of success.
When people name you, they preface their speech
With awe. It is simple to love a great man.
Remember then how hard it was to hate you!

Images of Love Rejected

When we two did not meet, it was
By choice, I choosing, you innocent,
In the dark. By choice, I sent
You out. You would have murdered
Me for love, sheeted the images.
There were no doors to keep the thief
Out and too many entrances.

I have made myself in seven years
A carpenter, can knock nail and stick
Together, live in my own shelter.
Muscles have grown you cannot tell,
Where the calf is strong, and here,
With work, the arm and wrist thick.

Looked back almost constantly,
You are the image, pin-point marker
Where love began. In my library
Your gifts of books remain; my cells
Divide, die, with your name locked in.
Psychologically, your body's

Mine. Because imagination
Will not stay separated
From love; like earth, will circle in-
Wards, joining land and water,
Without permission I've made you son,
Father, dear lover rejected.

Promises

All night your promise buried in my ear,
The seed in-rooting new life, new life.
Was it disappointment, the stuff
Of daily life I hear?
Believing such an easy thing, to lie
Is stupid, like children are stupid,
Cunning about their powers and led
By truthful desire to fantasy.
When too old to care, too young to regret
Anything overmuch, the taste of apples
Remains sweet. Promises tell of fables
I'm glad to hear and tomorrow will forget.
After work, after food and sleep, at thirty,
Glad to be startled by promise or lie.

Silence

Lightly you brush your hand against my hair,
In this gesture, too, careful.
And I, when I hold you, your bare
Chest beating like a clock against my ear,
It is to release you only.
Always we take pains to leave each other
Our acre of breathing space. Now that we lie,
For the moment content to lace fingers,
Cheek against cheek, in deep breathing
Together, I forget and speak out; then,
Chairs, tables, the wide ceiling
And long glass of the room which keeps
Night out, discomfort suddenly a woman
Caught naked before a strange man.
I come to where I prefer to guess at
Silence, that bare and careful quiet.

Divorce

While you sat certainly
On your bed, on your sofa,
By your work table, I
Fetched you food, etcetera,
To wait upon your, oh who knows?
Love. Each day strung on errands;
Each night, on hands and knees, so
Insistent on duty.

Some of your gifts I keep:
A dress for a birthday,
A cloth cat I sleep
With, a pretty purse.
Your battered ring I wear
And again put away.

What stays soonest to hand
Is the stuff of two years
Together and the bright
Edges of rare meetings.
My quarrel has little
To do with you. No, not even
When I drank a bottle
Of your best whiskey and cried
For mama. (I still cry
But know it is for me.)

Did you not see
A frightened child out
Looking for home and father?

You played so well at
The unloving figure,
And I nothing if not
A crying child. Separate,
At last, I know
Father will not come,
And if he will, I shall not
Let him in into my home.

Between Women

One day I shall write about you —
taller, tougher, curved Amazon
(you queened it in every show,
twelve-year-old woman, men like fleas
jumping into your skin-stretched pants;
queer pedigree, an empress chou
appalled by the hovelled family
under heel in the common bed:
brute and vulgar spirit as
only immigrant Hakkas have bred) —
and me, the stray dropping by,
with my mongrel tongue, to be burned
in the shadow of your assertive
flesh and flashy hair. But in my mind
the damned secret of seeing double,
fiction's poisoned perspective,
painted you in lesser colours
than mine. You have never forgiven
this. One day I shall write about us
when the cracked and acute glass
no longer shows your grimace
rivalled on my uncertain face.

Birth, Sex, Death

The three awesomes all down the road
somewhere; or, past encountering,
past imagining. The signal
boredom of the thing — boom, she says,
and boom, boom, boom. Each boom, now grown,
hurrying elsewhere. No time to
listen to old complaints. Oh, sex,
she says, nothing to it. Can't
even recall the look of it.
Not modern like you. The malice
as she takes in nylons, bras,
panties — such lovely things (but not
for her) — matted in noon rain like
silky pelts, dead animals. She
strokes pink, lavender satin. Lucky
girl! Looks sharp at him. Rich, rich,
what more can a woman want?
And she, so sad, had never got it.

Inventing Mothers

I bite the fluffy tissue.
Roses flurry from my mouth
in June, and wildlife memories
of other children's mothers
spring too: their scurrying fussy
ways, pecking rice-birds busy

in the drying fields, intent
on harvest. Child, I peeked at them
buried in hearts of houses,
flapping, like hearts that will not fail,
spare, efficient hands at pots
and foreheads, at thread and lots

of mending, heaps of broken
promises from the world, shattered
china cups, and fathers' thrashings.
They were not brusque like brothers
or miserly like old aunts. They
made breakfasts, washed, swept, and stayed

till next morning. A little friend's
prayerful mother was gaunt bone, mean.
It didn't matter. She blanched
cheeks, trained waist and hair, made ends
meet where nothing else would. She
put herself before misery.

so saved the children. Bruising
lips, I make tissues of roses,
flinging seedtime for my son,
coins, kites, parings, extravagances
of mothering, while the lies
of childhood, puckering, rise and rise.

In Cities, Some Old Women

Some old women, very old at sixty,
Seventy, eighty, can wink most mornings,
Say, "How do you do?" "Thank you,"
And mean it. Timid as mice,
They nibble affectionately,
Do their hair, drift, cluster like nice
Puffweeds where parks and benches, yew
Trees, pigeons, fly to receive them.

In cities, some old women are not grand-
Mothers or mothers. They have no problem
With identity; will see you
Buried before they turn in for the
Evening. Husbands, sons, daughters,
Lovers surrendered, they can cram
Toffees and sweets in the larder,
Finally keep clean kitchens, shutters,
Floors, finally live clean as a whistle
To scare away ghosts. They fear everything.

No one is so gentle or timely.
Their loneliness is gentleness,
Is clocks ticking never far till
Dawn from bedroom and deaf hearing.
If you were to keep them company,
They would cut hours into small pieces
Of cake, eat them greedily,
One by one, for tea and dinner.

A Woman Speaks of Grandchildren

I am tired of poetry —
this boring half-talking
to yourself half-asleep —
broken flight of women
turned unsuccessfully
to birds tumbling
into the deadly
arrogant ocean.
Instead I want
a pot of fragrant rice
to share with good mothers:
grow yeasty thighs and sit
comfortably on backside
five grandchildren at my feet.

It's terrible to be
seduced by filthy books
with high thoughts which make you want
to delete the world.
Thoughts that starve you,
eat your heart out,
use all feelings up
even those for yourself,
lock you in a room
from crowds and crying babies.
Mothers want to feel
babies against their rough cheeks,

to see each one of five
pinky fingers opening
regardless of sunlight
or of darkness.

Have you also wasted
your life in libraries,
walking between tall walls
of words and listening
to them conversing
with each other?
Deep talk — splendid
as a sea-king's palaces,
his oldest and newest, leaping
among giant sea-fronds —
and I've wanted to fly
from the dull silent rooms
up to the clear blue,
my own swift bird
in the heart
of light those books
described so well —
to blue thoughts spelling
among airy towers
in waves underwater.

But a little bird
I'll never be. No, let me fall
asleep among loud voices
of grandchildren grown tall
on milk and fragrant rice.

Adam's Grief, Eve's Fall

Grieving, no matter at how large a loss,
Is not enough. It is easy to cry
Since one first stood, dumb with rage and crossed
With grief, and wondered at water from his eyes.
It is where to go from there, with only
Strange plants and rocks, creatures indifferently
Shy or ravenous; how to live with his
Lights and dark occurring remorselessly,
With all voice withdrawn, excepting this:
Speech which is sufficient enterprise.

Suicide-Poet

Words plague you. Swarming like flies,
Their buzz crawls in your ears, eats your eyes,
And hides your extraordinary head.
Like Sad Sack you walk under
A personal cloud of disaster
In a constant shower of sufferings.
On an ordinary day
You encounter strange omens:
Domestic animals bleeding over
Common lawns; demented salesmen hover
On your doorsteps. Simple plants prick your thumb,
And you fall asleep among children
And husbands. Even your mother, dumb
Among the vacuum-cleaners, can't fathom
Your distortion. Sickness serves you
Well, makes you soft and rotten, able
At a glance to discriminate
In others lame and crippled.
Grown grim to the bone you say
What only death can forgive you.

Summer Seminars

I
Not idiot compassion, friend.
Working on age, growing woman
Before growing old. Bodies
Are love in making, open
To dactyls, hair, these slivers.

What damn nonsense. You would never listen.

The nuns spoke in your ear; their hoods
Are skin sheaves fluttering.
Bald Irish women hooded
In black dresses. Only their brows stood
Pink. You, Atman, breathe in my ear.
I hear you breathe, hear you side-wise
Spirit: Bodies are love in
Making. Practice this truth, young nun
In your tunic.
                    Your body is

Beautiful already withering,
Foaled and blown-bellied. Man
Dionysius rules in your head.
It was not woman you wanted.
I hear your pain. It is clear
It was not woman you wanted.
The grey plastic shades slap in the
Wind. No terrible dragons
Wait at the gate, grey skulking
Lover. I hear you breathe here where

My belly moves.
This is my first practice.

II
Teach me to grow old. You are
Growing old. You are fat. You are ugly.
Your legs are rose bushes. You are
Not my teacher, grammarian, ignus
Fatuus. I will speak loudly, assert
My pain. It does not hurt, the still
Centre: I will master, my eye will
Grow round. I will wash with
Pharmaceutical fluid, smell
Your presence, this living tissue.
I am learning with your help,
Without your help. It is all
Doubleness. Strange to grow
Fourteen with the children of
My friends.

III
I must speak like a man before
Grey hairs testify. Will I believe
What I believe? Your symbols are rocks.
No one said to climb them, to
Approach, to bury in another
Avalanche. You spoke from the heart.
Speaking gently you came through the door.
I thought I saw you, bald one,
Musician, raunchy and paunchy. I have
A headache, you said. The lightning
Was in the room. How unhappy!
You claimed the lightning, settling

In the black armchair like any
Jehovah. Man voice, the lightning
Spoke, It was the fury of
A long day, humidity of
Day breaking to night. There is no
Significance to the system.
Only the day claimed breaking water and heat.

IV
I have read the others. They also
Exist. They plain. They chatter.
I hear them on my arms picking
And plucking.
                    I have read you
Too deeply, wanting to forget
Cycle of generation. It is
Only another wheel.

Frau Frommer was wonderful.
Her mind ran like currents while
We ate her salad. I could not pay
Attention, worrying like a sister
On the nature of her sorrow.
But only like a sister. I read her
Too, the rivulets flowing through threnodies.
She was too complex to read
The woman surfacing for breath.
"I grow greedier," she said. "My branches
Reach out like a piano-player
But my arms are too short."
She was not a mirror mirroring
You; I did not fall asleep or
See a mirror in her house

156

Although the thunder continued
Till the room smelled of sulphur.
She was too busy thinking to
Read, but she thought on her reading.
She will be my teacher.

V

This pace is slow. There is no rocking
No knocking for tight seals. Steadily
I follow the steps of unraveling,
The lessons of reading, of holding, of
Knowing. You are only a person. You are
A nickel xerox, a sound in the sound-room,
A tune on the concertina playing
Guises, The ruse is to flatten
You, to put you on a page. The ruse
Is to flatten you in the passing,
In the passage that won't lie on a page.
The quick storm is raining now.
The sound is pleasing. Stop. Listen.
The light rain is pleasing. Sleep
With a sheet because of the cool.

VI

In the morning Nancy was a
Dandyeyed. You were a cloud.
You sat with your back to us
At the next table. I kept
Glimpsing the large head, neck of an
Ox. We talked of women, of men with
Women, you flashed into view
Your back turned to us. It was
Creepy having you there so

Sudden. You were zooming to your
Island. Only the ghost kept
Appearing, a vapour from breakfast,
A frog from the August swamps,
A voice ringing like coin on
Rubble, cunning ruined
Voices among red wheelbarrows.

The Business of Machines

The woman:
    It moves. I don't want to.
    She would not look into his eyes.
    It was business they
    Were there on together.
The stranger:
    Part your legs. Relax.
    It could have been a stone,
    A splinter curled. The shock
    Of her nature, almost forgotten,
    Showed still pacing, able to kill.
The story:
    It could have been funny.
    Or wicked. His machine took back
    The stone, the splinter, the mess
    On the floor. She was part
    Of a process of numbers.

The women napped on white cots
In long silent rows.

Birth

Lizard ran. Her path sped, packed,
Hot in mother sun's eye.
It ran stony, strong as her back.
Running slithery slide she ate
Purple-winged air. Lizard's mind
Flickered on her tongue, flash
Of dark mouth and light, wing-
Warm in tummy, swallowing.
Lizard hummed her mother's song:
The black water is blood, black
Air is vision. Red stones compel,
White stones grow. Mother, crack the shell!

A Dream of Duty

Nothing can be seen
till we acknowledge
the subtle woman's dream.
In fact, there is duty:
a clean house with shaken
rugs, oiled picture frames.
The woman moves among
glossy plants and tiles,
child and husband dusted
free of strange desires.
Here is my life, she says.
Behind the brightening
lamps evening falls
outside and the visitor
must let herself out.

Family Album

The boy stood cocky on his mother's knee:
Opaque image distilled in silver eye.
He knew as none did what it was to be.

Poised in elegance of infancy,
In folds of cloth and flesh, and gazing high,
The boy stood cocky on his mother's knee.

Worlds of chairs and sofas were his to see:
Warmth, motion, light, all mastered by his cry:
He knew as none did what it was to be.

What was his mother? Her vague history
Hardly recalled in sorrow, ravished by
Boy standing cocky on his mother's knee,

She knew the guarded yards outside, crazy
Dogs and hearts, mind locked behind sigh.
He knew as none did what it was to be.

Unlikely met, the lonely figure, she
Turns her half-face, bliss, suspicious eye,
While boy stood cocky on his mother's knee,
Knowing as none did what it was to be.

The Tent

Already he wants a tent with a door that locks.
The green-orange nylon squats, quadrant-like,
in a room of thick burgandy pile.
All the colors look right when a child's in the picture.
He lies on its blue mat, flap raised, while
I read him another fantastical chapter.
He doesn't know yet it's his life that's fantastical.
Soon he will sleep, mouth gaping, arms thrown wide,
against the heaved-up linens and quilt.
By morning he'll have kicked every cover aside.

Tomorrow he will find real doors that close,
filing cabinets with steel spring-loaded action,
a house standing in a field of strange houses,
each bearing chains, latches, locks, and dead-bolts
in a town whose name I'll not be able to pronounce.
His mouth will shut firmly — he'll want no mother's tale
to be picking his door! Children learn to prize
cover in a country of difficult solitude.
I shall keep his tent for myself. Its
skin will stretch lightly above my opened eyes.

Myopia

Walking in the dark carefully
so as not to wake the man in the bed
she walks into the door, and sits
two rooms away rubbing a nasty
swelling bruise over the startled
right eye. The pattern repeats
itself over and over again:
the female figure in the carpet
fumbling through the unlighted room.
Be noiseless as the night. Do not

wake the sleeping humans, round
as warm loaves full of breathing weight.
Your gliding self is silent, alerting
to an inviolate invisible.
Now, miserly caretaker, if I were your child,
would you be more forgiving,
would you pace from me gladly
as you do from husband and child,
furtive and guiltlessly abandoning?

Women's Dreams

Women spin dreams all hours of the day;
At night the naked light spits its light
On our hairy parts. The gay says,
You women do not know how to love.
Yes, wilfully we choose the ill-matched mate,
Delight in the effort to fit.
Being Mother Nature and our own creation.
Puzzles, tricks, strategems: we match wits
Because we have not know dominion.
Initiates balance breast and buttock,
Colour faces, depilate their arm-pits;
But, desperadoes on the run, they hatch
Bat-like in the furred, mammalian cave.
Women are crones still, clumsy magicians.
Even fat and ugly may stir a cock
And lord it for a day and a night.

I Look For Women

Mid-life stalled, I look for women.
Where are they, my mothers and sisters?
I listen for their voices in poems.
Help me. I've fallen asleep, fallen
With sleepers. These women have murdered
Themselves, violent, wrenched from home.

Grandmother was barren. She died,
Tubes in nose and green shanky arm,
Hair yellow, a dirty dye, patches
Like fungus on a stricken pine.

I read terrible stories —
Hate, rage, futilities of will —
And look for women, the small
Sufficient swans, showers of stars.

AFTERWORD

Tongue And Root:
Language In Exile

When my husband heard that I had been invited to speak at a symposium on writers in exile, he burst out bitterly, "But you are not in exile!"

Indeed for him, sharing a child and living in domestic quarters with me for over fifteen years, it is intolerable to think of me, his wife, as *someone who is not at home where she is*. The condition of exile is problematic not only for the individual who carries it with her, like a snail with its heavy horned shell, but for the people and country she claims to be exiled from and for the host family which nourishes and supports her in her impoverishment.

Exile immediately presupposes the sense of involuntary removal; it connotes dispossession, displacement, discontentment. As removal from an original and significant place, a homeland, an ancestral plot, it implies movement from inside, with the sense of wholeness, integrity, shelter, belonging, empowerment, to outside, with the multiple negative associations of being outcast, of ostracism, marginalization, estrangement, enfeeblement, rootlessness, disintegration, and loss. The original political use of the term, to punish a citizen by banishment from family, home, and social power to solitary existence among unfriendly strangers, persists today unambiguously, together with a host of new and modern permutations. It persists because the truth of state authoritarianism has not changed. From ancient Greek city-states to recently created African nations, politicians have strategically dispossessed their opposition, stripped them of the rights of citizenship, in order to enforce their own legitimacy and rule. In claiming exile, therefore, the individual is crying foul against a state; is asserting a condition of inequality and injustice at the hand of an oppressing force.

But now one reads of social scientists and historians defining such a thing as voluntary exile. Is voluntary exile the condition by which an individual chooses to remove himself from a centre from which he has already been excluded? If free choice is implied by the modifier, "voluntary," does that freedom extend to those conditions prevailing at the centre which lead inevitably to the hard road of departure? Or do we have in the phrase "voluntary exile" one of those remarkable ironies of the modern political consciousness, where one denies the reality of state aggression by positing the individual's power to escape or circumvent it?

As for me, I have for a long time seen myself as nothing but an individual. This self-image of "an individual" is the bottom of a descent, from nation and community. Growing up as a native-born Chinese Malaysian, I was surrounded by the solid structures of a large extended family, a narrow parochial convent education, a small-town tropical and pluralistic mentality, and the international English language. Nothing about my life was exotic or strange to me; the quiddities of normalcy are the sacred ground from which every writer begins. Nor was it odd that at the age of fifteen and sixteen, we Malacca children were asked to write essays in English on the meaning of democracy, on the topic of Malaysia for the Malaysians. Why should we doubt that our country was for us? We were in no way well-off, but as urbanized and English-educated students we anticipated a future which would include us and in which we were told repeatedly we would be the leaders of tomorrow.

If history were a process whereby expectations came true, perhaps it would have no place for exiles! That sense of destiny so casually instilled into my generation of Malaysians: where is it now? For the country has taken another path, another destination. The process of nation-building is never easy or harmonious, but for those whom it would exclude, it can never be acceptable without a struggle to influence it to larger, more integrative ends.

This struggle is waged by the parties in internal exile, by those whose contributions and services, and in like manner, whose rewards are denied in the present and future of the nation. These are the real heroes, who have not abandoned their vision of their place under the sun, and who daily live in the presence of political absence; their identities to be rendered invisible so as to enable the easier deprivation of their rights. When one group finds it difficult to stand up and say its name; when to say one's identity is already to mark one as lesser than, that is where the boundaries of exile begin.

Many English-language writers in Malaysia have found their foundations shifted in the last twenty years. Poised in 1957 with the attainment of independence to participate in the political fullness of nationhood, they have found instead historical definitions which exclude them. The only national literature, it is promulgated, is literature in the national language. This definition starkly underlines the movement to restrict national identity to a monocultural and monolinguistic position, a constitutional decision which cannot be debated under pain of imprisonment without habeas corpus. Indeed, for many English-language writers brought up to respect their country's constitution, this promulgation is a more effective silencer than tanks and barbed-wire. As a lover of one's country who cannot but wish good for its future, one must cut one's tongue off before one criticizes its law. And indeed I have little wish to criticize, for a newer and younger generation born without that particular sense of destiny that we were imbued with must be free to struggle with its evolution of nationhood. But as a free-floating individual, with my tongue still intact although my roots are cut, I can lament and record.

Andrew Graham-Yooll in an essay made a distinction between the whiners who had given up hope of returning to the homeland and those exiles filled with energy who worked surely towards the day of their return. Between the two groups, I am the whiner. Yet I can always return. The flight from New York where I now live to my home town would take no more than two days of steady travel. More separates me from my original place than distance. Educated to have my talents of service to my society, I know now that my particular linguistic talents are instead viewed as irrelevant to the official line on national development today. Proud of my abilities, I had seen myself when young as belonging to an intellectual and creative elite, helping to shape and create the features of this brave new pluralistic Southeast Asian world. Now the hour for that elite has been taken away, and another had taken up its position.

The unpleasant news about those in exile, whether internal or external, is that unless they overcome paralysis, history will be shaped without them. This exile, after all, has nothing in common with the metaphysical indulgences of individuals who disdain history in the light of existentialist perspectives. "Existence before essence" is all very well for a Frenchman who is so Eurocentrically positioned that from the bosom of his city and his language he dared play with ideas of nothingness and being. But for persons who in their lifetimes have found themselves acted upon so that their sense of selves, the essence of their cultural beings has become progressively denied and marginalized, their deracination is political first rather than philosophical and results from an assault on core identities, whether ethnic, racial, linguistic, or personal.

This assault was clearly formulated under colonial conditions. The suppression of education in the native languages in favour of English-language and British-subject education was a deliberate policy of the British colonial administrators whether in Ghana, India or Malaysia. Simultaneously there was a dismantling of traditional native social and economic structures, replaced by western laws and innovations of agricultural, industrial and mining ventures which would prove most profitable for western economic interests. The destruction and suppression of native customs, languages and economic structures, it is true, occurred together with the instruction in and replacement by western languages, customs, and economic structures. The many positive improvements in living standards (which are real and indisputable, such as better nutrition, improved medical care and water supplies, a more rational and equitable justice system) masked for a long time the many negative consequences of westernization on non-western peoples: the loss in cultural esteem, the empty aping of alien manners which filled in the vacuum after the loss of ancient traditions, the change from culture-production to culture-consumption and the consequent disintegration of social cohesion and communal values, and so on. Any individual coming from a colonial and post-colonial society, as most of the current professionals in Third World countries do, feels the force of these brief historical statements in her life.

Alienation to such an individual is not a philosophical abstraction but a political fact. For many Malaysians of my generation, the language we loved and were most at home in was not our mother tongue, be it Urdu or Hindi or Mandarin or Cantonese, but the tongue of the white man we were educated to fear and admire, English. The Irish nuns who taught me to read Tennyson, themselves children of colonialism, did their jobs well. I not only learned to

170

read, but I also learned to love; I not only learned to imitate, but I wished to belong. For this personal outcome it is not the Irish women I have to thank but the English language itself and its manifestations in literature.

Thus, when the colonial world came to an end in August 1957 in the then Federation of Malaya, I rejoiced in the emergence of my people into their moment of liberation; but I naively expected the sun never to set on the English language. In the quarrel between national identity, as defined by a monocultural and monolingual ideology, and the English language, I recognize that I am not only a whiner but a potential troublemaker. English is to much a part of my identity, confused as it already is ethnically, racially and culturally, that I cannot abandon it for any overriding purpose. Yet I do not believe in the hegemony of English in the international scene; I would always want the wonderful babble of poly-languages about me, for I grew up in a world where I spoke three languages and heard another ten on either hand. And perhaps like a duckling who was hatched in the presence of a cocker-spaniel and waddles in order to wag its non-existent imprinted tail, I waddle rather than romp my way through pages of English prose.

Still, for all that, English is my calling. I make my living teaching it to native speakers, I clean up the grammar of English professors, I dream in its rhythms, and I lose myself for whole hours and days in its words, its syntaxes, its motions and its muscled ideas. Reading it and writing it is the closest experience I have ever had to feeling infinity in my presence.

Idealizing the language, I do not mean to idealize the English-language user. A Filipino writer, explaining why he wrote in English despite the resurgence of Tagalog or Filipino, the national language, after the Philippines won its independence from the United States in 1952, said, "I did not choose the language; it chose me." Another Filipino writer defends his choice of English as a historical accident. Everywhere where colonial masters have left and brown and colored people have entered into the halls of parliaments and universities to rule themselves, English has remained as that accidental stain on a people's intelligence and spirit. Leaders can only hope to purify their tribes by sacrificing whole generations of educated intelligentsia; or they can attempt to contain the linguistic contagion by limiting mastery of it to a few privileged elect. In either case they are also condemning their societies to economically regressive and authoritarian measures. The Third-World English-language user is no historical anachronism or anomaly but the business man who desires increased profit, the scholar who wishes to increase his learning, the ordinary man or woman who would share in the goodness of freedom and individual liberty.

For while the English-language user may be motivated by subjective or selfish ends, he is grafting himself not only to a tree of language but to a larger history of human development. English is no longer that Anglo-Saxon-based speech of a few million people living on a small northern island off the Atlantic Ocean. English, in fact, has not been a national language of that kind for more than a century. It is, factually, a global language, the first of its kind; serving more than the needs of empire, unlike Latin; more than the prestige of that originating island nation. Right now, it serves the needs of every human whose understanding and imagination would overleap tribal and national boundaries. The student in Beijing who practices her English with tapes imported from Ohio; the Nigerian who studies for his O levels in his village-school; the Indian journalist who writes his copy in English while he interviews in Marathi; to these and many more, the English language is the means by which they communicate as a species. Independent nations today no longer see English as a tool of western imperialism but as a medium for trans-national species communication.

And yes, in the process of our discovering what we share with others, our tribal boundaries can become unstuck, our ancient or recent national identities can be shaken. This is the risk that Third-World English language writers take, the risk that all explorers come up against in travelling too far, the possibility of alienation from their native cultures, of losing one's way home. The child who leaves home, seduced by a stranger's tongue, and never returns is to be mourned for.

But exile presumes that such a child is forbidden to return. The language this child has learned is surrounded by an aura of illegitimacy, danger, and taboo. This rejection of their English-language writers, in India or Nigeria or Southeast Asia, can only damage those societies themselves. In denying a place for writers

172

who have attached themselves to a language tree other than the politically correct one, these societies are seeking to control the act of creativity at its very root. It is an attempt at social control which sets loose the worst tendencies towards cultural paranoia and authoritarianism and which destroys that which should be precious for young nations and ancient communities alike: the lyric voices of their free men and women celebrating their past and inventing their future.

We should all support nationalistic measures to recover and reconstruct that cultural self-esteem a colonial history has almost obliterated. However, to carry on a vendetta against English-language users is a dangerously divisive policy in countries where social cohesion is most necessary. More to the point, it is ultimately futile when ordinary citizens can see how the political elite are educating their children in English.

As for me, choosing to make my future with the language I love, I find, of course, that language is never enough. The whole of a person is of sights, sounds, smells, motions, tastes, a community of sensations we call country. The naming is in English, but now the objects for naming are no longer at hand. I do not wish to be in exile. To remain faithful to my origins, I must be unfaithful to my present. To be constant to my Malaysian identity, I must continue in the United States to be a stranger in a strange land. Still, I have a language in my hand. To me, it is a language where the idea of freedom is broader and stronger than it is in any country.

Shirley Geok-lin Lim
London, 1988

"Tongue and Root: Language in Exile" was published in Third World Affairs 1988, ed. Raana Gauher, Third World Foundation for Social and Economic Studies, London.

Two new titles from PROF. **SHIRLEY GEOK-LIN LIM** :

MONSOON HISTORY (UK £6.99, USA $11.99)
Poems selected from Modern Secrets & No Man's Grove with the comple
Crossing the Peninsula (winner of the 1980 Commonwealth Poetry Prize
"The poet in exile, but a counter-exile that permits an embracing of all
contradictions." World Literatures Today

WRITING S.E./ ASIA IN ENGLISH: Against The Grain (UK £12.99
USA $24.99)
The ten chapters demonstrate that South East/Asian Writing in English,
Against the Grain of local speech, national languages and national canons
have much to tell us about place and region, and also about the nations
that their imaginations press upon from the outside of linguistic borders.

Three from **K.S.MANIAM** :

THE RETURN (UK £5.99)
This novel of magical realism has become a Malaysian modern classic.
Ravi attempts to come to terms with himself by sustaining the classical
Hindu virtues of spiritual proportion, harmony and grace, and avoiding
the decay of ethnic civilization through his pursuit of social mobility.
"THE RETURN bids fair to take a place among the top two or three of
any published Malaysian/Singaporean fiction in English"
Ooi Boo Eng, Univ. of Malaya

IN A FAR COUNTRY (UK £5.99)
This post-modernist novel is a potent cocktail of cultures, race and
religions.
"The book seeks to free itself from the literary ghetto by addressing
national issues and departing from realism to do so."
Dr. Paul Sharrad, Univ. of Wollongong, Australia

SENSUOUS HORIZONS, four stories & four plays (UK £6.99, USA
$11.99)
The eight works explores the complex and varied lives of husbands, sons,
wives, and lovers, all players in a game as old as time.

N THE NAME OF LOVE by **Ramli Ibrahim** (UK £6.99)

This is daring theatre taking risks and living dangerously, reviving a spirit hat at the time subverts and affirms the cultural concerns it displays, uestioning and challenging, but never losing sight of that essential heatrical quality:entertainment. The plays mark a major contribution to outh East Asia theatre, and one which will delight audiences everywhere." rof. John McRae (Univ. of Nottingham)

VAYS OF EXILE by **Wong Phui Nam** (UK £5.99)

his collection traces the development of the poet from student days to arly maturity in lyrical litany, honouring the Malaysian soul as well as the eographical and spiritual ground of his country.

Wong's poetic scenario is eschatological in that it discovers powerful estructive forces at work in the natural and social world." Anne Brewster, owards a Semiotic of Postcolonial Discourse

S I PLEASE by **Salleh Ben Joned** (UK £6.99, USA $11.99)

Anybody who wants to understand cultural politics today should read this ook. Anybody who wants to understand Malaysia today should read this ook. And anybody who wants an insight into the confrontations of East nd West, of Islam and the secular or Christian world, should read this ook!" Margaret Drabble

KOOB PACIFICA ANTHOLOGY

NO.1. *S.E. ASIA WRITES BACK !* (UK £5.99)

No.2. *THE PEN IS MIGHTIER THAN THE SWORD* (UK £6.99, USA 11.99)

he principle of Postmodern/Postcolonial writing is to deviate from the radition and to develop a new direction of thought...The understanding of writer involves anamnesis in the psychoanalytical context, the free ssociation of ideas and imagery of the unconscious in situations past to liscover the hidden meanings of his life.

The Skoob Pacifica Series has provided a means for many writers to reach nternational readership...The Pacific Rim should not be seen just for its conomic importance but also for the emergence of writings in English that all for recognition in the literary world." British Council, Literature Matters

SHANGRI-LA
HOTELS *and* RESORTS

SUPPORTING THE LITERATURES OF THE PACIFIC RIM

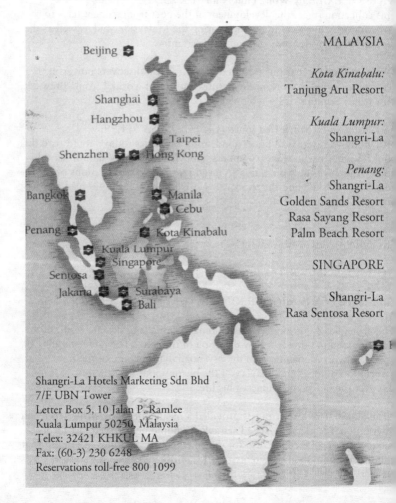

MALAYSIA

Kota Kinabalu:
Tanjung Aru Resort

Kuala Lumpur:
Shangri-La

Penang:
Shangri-La
Golden Sands Resort
Rasa Sayang Resort
Palm Beach Resort

SINGAPORE

Shangri-La
Rasa Sentosa Resort

Shangri-La Hotels Marketing Sdn Bhd
7/F UBN Tower
Letter Box 5, 10 Jalan P. Ramlee
Kuala Lumpur 50250, Malaysia
Telex: 32421 KHKUL MA
Fax: (60-3) 230 6248
Reservations toll-free 800 1099